GALVESTON
PLAYGROUND OF THE SOUTHWEST

Linda: Enjoy Galveston's Playground!

4-25-14

Jami Durham

4·25·14

Photo gallery booths located within Galveston's bathhouses were popular with beach visitors. This c. 1908 photograph of three children was taken by Louis Tobler, a Russian immigrant who operated photo gallery booths at the Pagoda, Murdoch's, and Breakers bathhouses before opening his own photo gallery, the Electric Studio, in the 1930s. (Courtesy of Galveston Historical Foundation's Preservation Resource Center.)

ON THE FRONT COVER: An early-19th-century traffic jam can be seen gathering around Murdoch's Bathhouse in this c. 1915 photograph, taken from the rooftop of the Hotel Galvez. (Courtesy of Galveston Historical Foundation's Preservation Resource Center.)

ON THE BACK COVER: Susan Norman and Ann DeWolfe relax on their inflatable FUNFLOTES in this c. 1950s promotional postcard advertising "FUNFLOTES sold at local sporting goods stores." (Courtesy of Galveston Historical Foundation's Preservation Resource Center.)

GALVESTON
PLAYGROUND OF THE SOUTHWEST

W. Dwayne Jones and Jami Durham

Published by Arcadia Publishing
Charleston, South Carolina

Printed in the United States of America

Library of Congress Control Number: 2012947339

For all general information, please contact Arcadia Publishing:
Telephone 843-853-2070
Fax 843-853-0044
E-mail sales@arcadiapublishing.com
For customer service and orders:
Toll-Free 1-888-313-2665

Visit us on the Internet at www.arcadiapublishing.com

To Sally Wallace, Burke Evans, and the founders of Galveston Historical Foundation who opened the door to heritage tourism in Galveston with their vision of the island's history and architecture one day becoming a major part of the city's economy.

CONTENTS

ACKNOWLEDGMENTS

Galveston: Playground of the Southwest offers a glimpse of the island's rich heritage of tourism and recreation. Many of us grew up coming to Galveston in the late 20th century when the industry had matured and the city abounded with tourist courts, motels, seafood restaurants, and beach venues. For some of us, the heritage tourism of the 1960s and 1970s introduced us to our lifelong profession of preserving buildings and interpreting museums. As authors, we wanted to capture some of the mental images we remember and show them through photographs, postcards, souvenirs, and memorials as we illustrate the evolution of the tourism industry in Galveston.

This publication is not intended to be the definitive history of tourism in Galveston. It is a fun and thought-provoking exploration that anyone can enjoy. Through the course of developing this book, we combed through countless photograph collections, begged our friends and colleagues to share, discovered hidden images collected by men and women far away, and drew from a number of regional repositories of history. The hard part of choosing the best images and writing the broadest narrative soon followed. In the end, the book is at least an introduction that may send you off to find your own family photographs of standing on the beach, leaving on a cruise line, or reeling in the largest catch of the day on the Galveston docks.

The majority of photographs appear courtesy of the Galveston Historical Foundation's Preservation Resource Center. The authors personally thank the Howard Robbins family, Christie Perfelto, Tom Greene, Eloise Powell, the Gaido family, Scott and Holley Hanson, Fred Huddleston, Karen Kremer, Adrienne and Michael Culpepper, Bob Morris, Tim Gould, Dr. Eric Avery, and the Dona Tucker Barker family for sharing their private collections of Galveston images.

Other collections noted within include: The Verkin Photo Company Collection, Dolph Briscoe Center for American History, University of Texas at Austin; Galveston County Museum; De Golyer Library, Southern Methodist University, Dallas; Auburn University Libraries, Auburn, Alabama; Houston Metropolitan Research Center; Library of Congress; Brazoria County Museum; San Jacinto Museum of History Association; Dallas Historical Society; and the Center for 20th Century Texas Studies, Galveston.

The authors especially thank Melody Smith and the Galveston Island Convention and Visitors Bureau, Brian Davis, Denise Alexander, David Canright, Will Wright, and all of the staff and board of directors of the Galveston Historical Foundation for their continued support, encouragement, and dedication to preserving the island's history and architecture.

A final thank-you is extended to the tourists and explorers of Galveston's rich playground. Your adventures keep Historic Galveston Island growing and developing with more vacation opportunities and the building of new family legacies.

INTRODUCTION

Galveston seems a natural for tourism. Surrounded by water, lined with long beaches, offering a quantity of historic and architectural attractions, and today dotted with accommodations and dining opportunities, the island city would become known as the "Playground of the Southwest." While a friendly debate over whether Galveston was a "treasure island" or a "pleasure playground" ensued throughout the 20th century, the images of Galveston that spread across the pages of publications distributed in the Southwest United States were appealing to tourists. The appeal grew so strong in the course of the 20th century that by the last half of the century, tourism had become a standard part of the Galveston and regional economy.

If you look back at the island's history, Galveston leaders built a local economy first from the natural harbor, developing and promoting a port, then by managing a railroad from the mainland into the port, making it a more viable part of the economy with cotton exports, and then, in time, a port for passengers to leave and arrive in Galveston. The medical school followed in the late 19th century as did other industries of finance and insurance. Certainly in Galveston's earliest days, the owners of the Galveston City Company saw no reason to promote the island for any other purposes than those already mentioned. By the end of the 19th century, however, tourism had begun to evolve as a viable part of many communities in the United States. As the concept of leisure time became a part of the lifestyles of many wealthy Americans and Europeans, destination travel—meaning the movement from one geographical location to another for rest, education, and relaxation—became an economic endeavor. Galvestonians with access to leisure time themselves would grasp this idea and bring it home to the island.

Despite the relatively slow development of the tourism industry in the 19th century, Galvestonians long valued the Gulf waters in the warmest months and made the expansive stretches of beach a playground for swimming and gathering shells. Women and children lingered on the beach by day, and men often took to the waters for swimming in the evening. The rough-packed sand provided good traction for the bicycles, carriages, and horses and opened up recreation of these typically utilitarian vehicles with friendly races and outings on the beach. Active recreation along the beach was an everyday occurrence but became an issue for single men after 1860. At that point, during and after the Civil War, the city began to craft new ordinances to ensure the proper use of the beach as well as aspects of civil decorum and behavior. In 1865, the first of the city ordinances prohibiting nude beach bathing during daylight hours was posted, and in 1877, the city passed an ordinance requiring bathers to be covered from "neck to knee." Both of these ordinances foretold the coming of a public appreciation of the beach and a growing abundance of free social time.

In 1860, the Galveston Houston & Henderson Railroad, under the leadership of its president, James Moreau Brown, the owner of Ashton Villa, completed the first railroad bridge connecting the island with the mainland. The rail line during the Civil War was mainly used for commerce and some military positioning, both directed toward the harbor. After the war, people began to arrive on the railroad on excursion trips from other cities in Texas. Rail travel for tourism grew in time and expanded to include an active interurban rail system for the greater Houston area. In addition to the rail lines, oceangoing vessels grew at the same time and brought visitors to the island from around the globe.

In the late 19th century, souvenir and trade booklets promoted Galveston first for commerce and second for tourism. Striking photographs of the island showcased beautiful Victorian houses, streets of oleanders, prosperous industries, social and recreational venues, and an idyllic setting for all to live or visit. While these publications cast a magical eye on Galveston Island, the distribution attracted visitors and began a nascent but substantial local investment in tourism. The intersection of the beach and Twenty-fifth Street became a terminal for visitors taking the trolley to the beach. Glamorous hotels and entertainment venues sprang up, and the opportunities to enjoy the Gulf water grew.

The 1900 hurricane changed the economy and lifestyles of Galvestonians forever. As the island recovered and reconsidered its economy, local leaders and government agencies constructed the seawall that would become a major character-defining aspect of Galveston and a practical and economic opportunity for tourism. By 1906, the first portion of the seawall was finished and bathhouses, arcades, hotels, and various other amusements ran for five miles down the Boulevard.

In 1911, the Hotel Galvez opened and was soon known as "The Queen of The Gulf." In 1912, the city and county constructed the first concrete causeway and Galveston Island was linked for the first time with automobile transportation. Around the same time, trains and the regular interurban line were regularly bringing day-trippers to the island for rest and recreation. By the 1920s, "auto tourists" or "autoists" flocked seasonally to the island, filling its motels and restaurants and lingering on the beaches. Some of these tourists came for special events created to draw them here while other visitors were entertained with a vice triad of prostitution, gambling, and prohibited liquor. It was this darker side of tourism that made Galveston famous or rather notorious.

The most significant road building for Galveston began in 1946 with the construction of the Gulf Freeway. Completed in 1952, the two-hour travel time from Houston to Galveston was cut in half. This essential link to a larger regional economy opened the island to a regular stream of tourists year-round but especially in its summer season. In 1956, the Texas Rangers brought an end to the illicit triad and Galveston was left with its beach, its climate, and its collection of Victorian architecture.

Galveston continues to develop the tourism economy. Public debates frequently ensue on what is the appropriate direction. Some advocate for gambling and casinos, others for more passive forms of tourism, including the beaches, special events, and heritage tourism. Accommodating tourists, providing new entertainment venues, preserving historic buildings and areas like the Strand, and creating an acceptable beach environment are all part of the ongoing vision of Galveston's tourist economy. In the summer of 2012, the new Historic Pleasure Pier opened to impressive crowds. This new venue combined more than 100 years of focused tourism on several things: the beach, entertainment, and heritage. Interesting enough, the Pleasure Pier reuses a 1940 plan for tourism by rebuilding on the city's pier and locates similar attractions at almost the same location selected in the late 19th century, the intersection of Twenty-fifth Street (Rosenberg) and the beach.

Galveston's discussion of tourism will doubtlessly continue into the future. Perhaps new attractions will appear and from time to time old ones pass away. The basic ingredients of Galveston's tourism, however, will most likely remain or in a practical sense should be preserved and enhanced. The beaches, surrounding waters of the Gulf of Mexico and Galveston Bay, and our rich history and architecture will be key to Galveston's vitality and economic well-being into the 21st century.

Three ladies in winter coats and hats pose under Murdoch's Bathhouse. A sign advertising the photo gallery inside can be seen on the right, c. 1925. (Courtesy of Galveston Historical Foundation's Preservation Resource Center.)

Three men try their luck at landing a tarpon off Galveston's seawall—always an "exciting sport," as this postcard declares. (Courtesy of Library of Congress.)

With the completion of the Gulf Freeway in 1952, the two-hour travel time between Houston and Galveston was cut in half. Day-trippers were able to make the drive after church on Sunday, spending an afternoon enjoying the island's beaches and breezes. (Courtesy of Galveston Historical Foundation's Preservation Resource Center.)

The beach lay at sea level in the late 19th century and looking west from about Twenty-seventh Street offered an unobstructed view of the Gulf of Mexico and the community. Galveston beachgoers could rent a small-frame, gable-roofed cart for the day to change clothes, drag down into the surf, and escape the summer sun. Several await rental on the right side of the photograph. (Courtesy of Galveston Historical Foundation's Preservation Resource Center.)

Here again is the cover image seen in full. Murdoch's Bathhouse is the oldest named beach attraction, although the current building is new following Hurricane Ike in 2008. The original 19th-century building consisted of a raised set of walkways and long rooms with many open windows. It was a popular viewing pavilion and so well recognized that it offered advertising to the railroad companies. (Courtesy of Galveston Historical Foundation's Preservation Resource Center.)

This busy scene captures the flocks of visitors enjoying Galveston's many seaside "playground" amenities. (Courtesy of Library of Congress.)

OPPOSITE: By the 1880s, Galveston attracted national attention with its prosperous port and bustling economy. Souvenir booklets promoted the city as a favorable business environment and a destination for the growing leisure time. In the far upper right of this bird's-eye view, the beach attractions and bathhouses are visible at the juncture of Twenty-fifth Street and the Gulf of Mexico. (Courtesy of Galveston Historical Foundation's Preservation Resource Center.)

TOURISM IN THE 19TH CENTURY

Galveston of the mid- to late 19th century seemed a paradise: a low-scale urban community concentrated on the easternmost end of a barrier island and centered on the northern side near the natural port. These concentrations of buildings left the southern boundary along the Gulf of Mexico undeveloped and open to the sea for the daily use of residents and occasional recreation of visitors. The western end of the island remained barren, allowing for hunting, fishing, and recreational boating in the bay. At various times, local entrepreneurs would create some new attraction or concept to lure visitors or residents away from their daily work, but most of these were short-lived. As the after-work leisure time increased to allow recreational activities and the wealth of the community grew, the sites where tourists could enjoy Galveston increased both in number and in scope. Lavish beach pavilions faced the cool breezes off the Gulf of Mexico and gave pause in the heated days of summer. Some residents built fishing businesses in popular locations along the waterfront, with piers and other accommodations.

It may be best to describe Galveston tourism in this period of the late 19th century as one evolving into a more modern tourist industry rather than one that was fully developed. As the idea of leisure time changed, visitors began to expect businesses that catered to them. Entrepreneurs created small businesses along the beachfront with two examples being the offering of carts that rolled into the surf and renting bicycles that could be ridden on the hard sand. Other businessmen invested in major hotels and pavilions. During this period, the first major Victorian hotels and bathhouses appeared, representing some of the finest local architecture. Most of these entrepreneurs speculated that Galveston would

grow as a tourist destination. It did grow with a steady increase in seasonal visitors who partook of the Gulf water and the entertainment venues.

By 1900, it would be hard to say that tourism was recognized as a major industry or even a sizeable part of the local economy. There are relatively few statistics that can decisively determine the economy's makeup during the final years of the late 19th century. Despite that, the images and city maps that remain from the period indicate a shift in the development of the island toward the Gulf of Mexico. Galveston in these years also remained one of the largest communities in Texas.

In the early months of 1900, island residents continued to develop the city into a major business center for the state. Henry Rosenberg's gift to the island of the Texas Heroes Monument at Twenty-fifth Street and Broadway, dedicated in May 1900, shows the island's interest in creating grand boulevards and the national City Beautiful movement. On September 8, 1900, however, the great hurricane rolled across Galveston Island. The physical devastation was surmounted only by the large loss of life, making it still the single largest loss of human life from a natural disaster in the nation's history. In the trembling days and months that followed the hurricane, Galvestonians reconsidered almost every aspect of existence as a city and business center. The recommitments to the island began to become evident and the rebuilding started immediately. In this aftermath, the importance of tourism to Galveston's economy and physical setting would soon change. Galvestonians held a new respect for the massive Gulf waters and returned its interests to modifying the island with a seawall and grade raising and then using the newfound physical amenities as a destination for tourists.

Harper's Weekly (1895) illustrated Galveston's beach looking east from about Twenty-seventh Street and the Gulf of Mexico. The illustration shows late-19th-century bathing attire, the small beach carts rented by the day, and the ever popular bathhouses. (Courtesy of Galveston Historical Foundation's Preservation Resource Center.)

THE BEACH AT GALVESTON, TEXAS.—DRAWN BY W. P. SNYDER.

By the 1890s, Galvestonians walked the beach year-round. The woman, child, and dog in this photograph are enjoying the beach on a winter day. A cyclist is making tracks in the sand along the surf, another way to see the Gulf. (Courtesy of Dallas Historical Society.)

These two girls are picking up seashells along the beach during winter. While most visitors to the island came in the summer months by the late 19th century, some enjoyed the beach all year. In the background is the Pagoda pavilion covered in ample advertising for the Katy Railroad. (Courtesy of Dallas Historical Society.)

The Pagoda pavilion extended into the Gulf allowing guests a place to sun or fish. Bathers could climb down ladders or walkways to enter the water. It attracted visitors with its large domed roofs over a long gable-roofed walkway with windows set parallel to the beach. Vertical stripes highlighted each dome, and a cresting decorated the roof line. This pavilion lay just to the east of Murdoch's and was also raised over the Gulf waters. (Courtesy of Galveston Historical Foundation's Preservation Resource Center.)

This image of Murdoch's Bathhouse shows Galvestonians taking a carriage on the beach and riding horseback, both common ways to explore the 19th-century beach. (Courtesy of Galveston Historical Foundation's Preservation Resource Center.)

Murdoch's attracted many visitors in the height of summer season and became an excellent venue for Galveston restaurants. The Bon Ton Restaurant was a popular downtown establishment that offered a branch at the pavilion called Bon Ton Restaurant on the Sea. The proprietors offered open-air dining with tablecloths and fine cooking, especially the latest fish from the Gulf. (Courtesy of Galveston Historical Foundation's Preservation Resource Center.)

The Electric Pavilion became the earliest major beach attraction when constructed in 1881 by the Galveston City Railway Company. The company devised a plan to draw visitors by rail to the city and beach with an amusement gallery and bathing facility at Twenty-third Street and the Gulf. Designed by Nicholas Clayton, the wood-frame building with oversized "cathedral-like" towers lit up at night with what is believed to be the first use of electric lights in Texas. (Courtesy of Holley and Scott Hansen, Private Collection.)

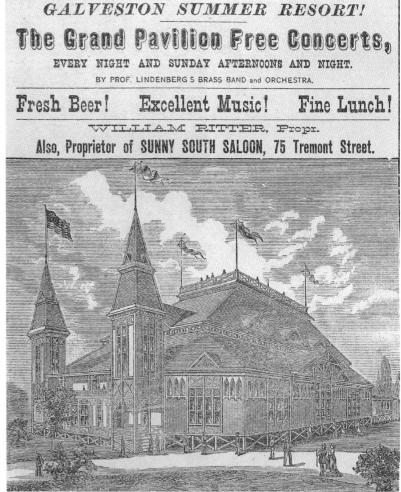

An advertisement for the Electric Pavilion in the 1881 *Galveston City Directory* enticed visitors with free concerts, fresh beer, and fine lunches. (Courtesy of Galveston Historical Foundation's Preservation Resource Center.)

The Electric Pavilion proved popular for two years before burning on August 1, 1883. Crowds gathered at the building to experience the beach and see performances like the high-wire walker in the upper right of the image. (Courtesy of Galveston Historical Foundation's Preservation Resource Center.)

Nicholas Clayton designed a second building at Twenty-third Street and the beach that opened on July 4, 1883. This sprawling wood-frame building is considered among Clayton's most spectacular Victorian designs. The Beach Hotel was a significant part of Galveston's skyline with its massive central tower and highly articulated roof features of gable dormers and striped roof shingles. Open porches led around the building with large windows punctuating each hotel room. Owned by William H. Sinclair, it proved a popular site for visitors and locals enjoying the beach. Within a few months of its construction, the hotel exceeded expectations for occupancy and became a year-round facility, improving Galveston as a destination. The hotel burned in 1898 and would not be matched by another beachside hotel until the Hotel Galvez opened in 1911. (Courtesy of Galveston Historical Foundation's Preservation Resource Center.)

The beach was the main attraction for Galveston visitors in the late 19th century and was for many their first encounter with the Gulf of Mexico. Professional photographers set up venues near the beach to capture the special outings of friends and family. These photographs often have a hand-painted backdrop that made the subjects appear to be on the beach in a relaxed pose. (Both, courtesy of Galveston Historical Foundation's Preservation Resource Center.)

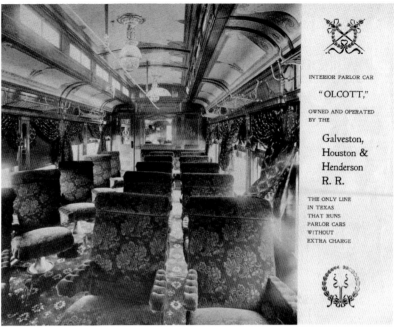

The Galveston Houston & Henderson Railroad used luxury parlor cars for passengers coming to Galveston. While the railroads vastly improved Galveston's attraction for leisure visitors, ships became an increasingly popular way for travel in the late 19th century as well. The Mallory Line, headquartered in New York, established the first of the great passenger vessels using Galveston's port. The early Mallory ships used steam power and called at such ports as Key West and New York. (Courtesy of Galveston Historical Foundation's Preservation Resource Center.)

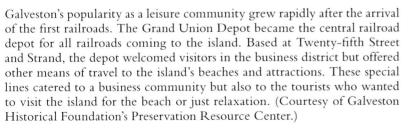

Galveston's popularity as a leisure community grew rapidly after the arrival of the first railroads. The Grand Union Depot became the central railroad depot for all railroads coming to the island. Based at Twenty-fifth Street and Strand, the depot welcomed visitors in the business district but offered other means of travel to the island's beaches and attractions. These special lines catered to a business community but also to the tourists who wanted to visit the island for the beach or just relaxation. (Courtesy of Galveston Historical Foundation's Preservation Resource Center.)

Galvestonians looked for other forms of recreation and entertainment other than the beaches. Charles Woollam created Woollam's Lake from one of the many bayous broken into the island. Streetcars or carriages provided transportation to the venue at the corner of Forty-first Street and Avenue Q. This oasis lay just beyond the residential neighborhoods and offered a quiet and contemplative setting. (Courtesy of Galveston Historical Foundation's Preservation Resource Center.)

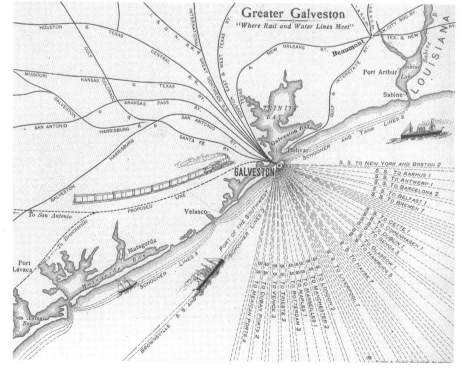

At the turn of the 19th century, Galveston Island entered a new phase of community development where tourism helped define the city. The concept of a "greater Galveston" played on its already established history as a railroad center and port. This graphic illustrates how Galveston was the point where land and water met. (Courtesy of Galveston Historical Foundation's Preservation Resource Center.)

This image captures the tragic hours following the September 8, 1900, hurricane. The photograph shows the debris line southeast of the Walter and Josephine Gresham house at Fourteenth Street and Broadway Boulevard. The photograph is from the Gresham family and may have been taken by one of the members living in the house in 1900. (Courtesy of Eloise Powell, Private Collection.)

Boulevard and Breakers Bath House,
Galveston, Tex.

This image captured about 1908 shows a brick street in front of the Breakers bathhouse. A fence separates the sidewalk and street, though both are used by pedestrians. A small sign at the end of the Breakers advertises getting a photograph taken and placed on a postcard. (Courtesy of Galveston County Museum.)

OPPOSITE: The beach and the seawall became a popular location for strolling in dress attire. This photograph shows the narrow top of the seawall, with its riprap of granite boulders along the eastern end before a wider sidewalk was added to allow promenading. Small sand dunes appear at the street level before the boulevard is completed. (Courtesy of Galveston Historical Foundation's Preservation Resource Center.)

THE SEAWALL AND AUTO TOURISM

The 1900 hurricane changed the economy and lifestyles of Galvestonians forever. As the island recovered and reconsidered its economy, local leaders and government agencies constructed the seawall that would become a major character-defining aspect of Galveston and a practical as well as economic opportunity for tourism. By 1906, the first portion of the seawall was finished and bathhouses, arcades, hotels, and various other amusements soon ran several miles down the boulevard. Galveston leaders promoted the island as the "Atlantic City of the South." A 45-foot-high sign at Seawall Boulevard and Twenty-fifth Street, lit by more than 5,000 lights, spelled out "Galveston the Treasure Island of America." Murdoch's Bathhouse at Twenty-third Street was three stories high and included a casino, a bathhouse, and the first Gaido's restaurant. Across the street, the Crystal Palace was built in 1916 and offered gambling, dancing, restaurants, penny arcades, and an indoor saltwater pool filled every night by high tide.

At Seawall Boulevard and Twenty-fourth Street, the Electric Park and the Galveston Amusement Company opened in 1906. Its rides, attractions, stages, performances, outdoor theaters, and restaurants brought midweek excursion trains from Houston. In May 1906, the *Galveston News* called the Electric Park the "Coney Island of the South." The seawall boasted many dance clubs as well. The Balinese, which jutted out over the Gulf, was originally called the Grotto while nearby was the Garden of Tokio, where dancers could enter to win cash prizes. In 1911, the Hotel Galvez opened and was soon known as "The Queen of the Gulf."

In 1912, city, county, and state officials finished the first concrete causeway and Galveston Island was linked for the first time with a national

network of automobile transportation. When the causeway opened, Texas governor Oscar B. Colquitt led more than 1,500 cars down Broadway Boulevard to Seawall Boulevard at Sixth Street and up Seawall to the Galvez. Around the same time, trains and the regular interurban line were regularly bringing day-trippers to the island for rest and recreation.

The concrete bridges and improved roadways brought an increasing number of automobile tourists to Galveston. By the 1920s, "auto tourists" flocked seasonally to the island, filling its motels and restaurants and lingering on the beaches. Some of these tourists came for special events created to draw them here like auto-racing, beauty contests, and carnivals. Other visitors were entertained with a vice triad of prostitution, gambling, and prohibited liquor. It was this darker side of tourism that made Galveston famous or rather notorious.

The most significant road building for Galveston began in 1946 with the construction of the Gulf Freeway. Completed in 1952, the two-hour travel time from Houston to Galveston was cut in half, opening the island to a regular stream of tourists year-round. In 1956, the Texas Rangers brought an end to the illicit triad and methodically closed the bawdy houses and the casinos. Galveston was left with its beach, its climate, and its collection of Victorian architecture, the latter providing Galveston with a new pathway for tourism during the 1960s.

Prior to the 1920s, most tourists to Galveston arrived by train, reaching the depot at Twenty-fifth Street and Strand then transferring to the trolley and most often heading to the beach. Hotel accommodations on the Gulf side of the island opened from the late 19th century through the early 20th century. The popularity of the automobile, however, shifted the most popular mode of transportation and opened the island up to thousands of new tourists. By the early 1920s, Galveston could be reached from the mainland on the north by a modern causeway and later by an automobile ferry from Bolivar Peninsula on the east end. The almost overnight increase in tourism created a demand for accommodations that grew into a sizeable industry. Auto tourists, or "autoists" as the literature of the day sometimes referred to them, sought a variety of accommodations from rustic camp settings to eventually small rooms at larger hotels and motels.

As the 20th century matured, accommodations reflected modern design trends, grew in number, and would cover most of the south side of the island from Sixty-first Street to the far east end. The hotels of the 1980s and more recent decades reflect a national trend to being resort complexes offering meeting spaces, banquet rooms, exotic pools and restaurants, and attractions that far exceed those of the early days. The automobile, however, remains the most consistent form of transportation to the island with new causeways being built and the continuation of the ferry.

Within a few years of the completion of the seawall, Galvestonians recognized the flexibility of the seawall as a boardwalk similar to Atlantic City. This view shows the newly built Breakers bathhouse and a wide sidewalk with a balustrade. The latter is long removed from the seawall. (Courtesy of Galveston Historical Foundation's Preservation Resource Center.)

Family photographers shot this group under Murdoch's on the beach. These stylish outfits reflect their interest in nautical themes. (Courtesy Mardi Mitchell, Private Collection)

078031, SEA WALL AND BEACH, GALVESTON, TEXAS.   COPR. DETROIT PUBLISHING CO.

This amazing photograph captures tourists at the seawall and beach in the 1910s. (Courtesy of Library of Congress.)

By 1910, the boulevard was in place, allowing carriages and automobiles to access the beach. This image shows the Breakers and Murdoch's Bathhouses in the background. Four modes of transportation from the early 20th century are visible in the photograph: walking, biking, carriage riding, and the automobile. (Courtesy of Galveston County Museum.)

In 1912, city, county, and state officials finished the first concrete causeway and Galveston Island was linked for the first time with a national network of automobile transportation. When the causeway opened, Texas governor Oscar B. Colquitt led more than 1,500 cars down Broadway Boulevard to Seawall Boulevard at Sixth Street and up Seawall to the Galvez. (Courtesy of Library of Congress.)

This passenger train is shown crossing the causeway c. 1908. (DeGolyer Library, Southern Methodist, University, Dallas, Texas, Ag2009.0005)

Tourists began to use the train as a means of visiting the island for its beaches and soothing climate. (Courtesy of Brazoria County Museum.)

This early view of the seawall shows the riprap of granite boulders along the eastern end of the structure. In the background are the early buildings of the medical school. (Courtesy of Galveston Historical Foundation's Preservation Resource Center.)

Murdoch's Bathhouse soon became a seawall icon at Twenty-third Street, sheltering bathers along its south side. Tourists interested in entering the water could rent a swimsuit, walk down a ramp to the water, and be in a controlled area. (Courtesy of Center for 20th Century Texas Studies.)

This image shows the controlled swimming area in the Gulf below Murdoch's Bathhouse. A safety line extends across the water and a lifeguard stand rises above the water about 15 feet. (Courtesy of Tom Green, Private Collection.)

Three lifeguards pose for a photograph around 1909. The medal, whistle, and chain around the neck identified them as official lifeguards.

Tourists of the early 20th century dressed well to visit the beach, indicating its acceptance as a community meeting place. The above image shows swimmers in the background, but a popcorn vendor is in the forefront wearing a white jacket. He can also be seen in the image below, near the foot of the staircase leading from the seawall down to the beach. (Both, courtesy of DeGolyer Library, Southern Methodist University, Dallas, Texas, Ag20005.0001.)

An interior photograph of the Electric Park faces south toward the seawall and shows a wooden bridge over one of the canals for the grade raising. The children on horseback are crossing the bridge. The roller rink with open windows is behind, and the electric swing is in the distance. (Courtesy of Dolph Briscoe Center for American History, University of Texas at Austin.)

This very early panorama was taken near the intersection of the new Seawall Boulevard and Twenty-fifth Street c. 1906. At the center of the photograph are the electric swing and a grandstand. Both became central attractions to the Electric Park. (Courtesy of the Library of Congress.)

This panoramic photograph taken in almost the same location in c. 1909 shows a nearly complete Electric Park. The image features the beginnings of the amusements offered by Galveston to attract tourists. The Electric Park consisted of a complex of wood-frame buildings, amusement rides, carnival-type features, and animal shows. (Courtesy of the Library of Congress.)

This view of the Electric Park, probably taken from Murdoch's Bathhouse, shows the vertical members of the electric swing and the roof of the carousel. (Courtesy of Galveston Historical Foundation's Preservation Resource Center.)

A clever ride called Shooting the Chutes sat on the western side of the Electric Park. It seems similar to later water rides with passengers placed in a "canoe like" cart. In the background is the castle and Tours of the World exhibit. (Courtesy of Galveston County Museum.)

An interior shot of the Electric Park shows the elevated grandstand with dome roof. In the background is the Ferris wheel. A sign for ice-cream cones points to another interesting attraction called the Human Laundry. (Courtesy of Galveston Historical Foundation's Preservation Resource Center.)

The electric swing became the centerpiece to the park. This vertical ride moved large baskets with passengers in a circle, dropping near the ground on large chains. (Courtesy of Galveston Historical Foundation's Preservation Resource Center.)

At night, the Electric Park earned its name. The park opened in 1906 and demonstrated the use of electric lightbulbs in clever and creative ways. The electric swing became the centerpiece to the park, proving to be a popular ride but even more interesting as a nighttime photograph. The swinging chains carrying baskets with passengers were dazzling for spectators to watch. (Both, courtesy of Galveston Historical Foundation's Preservation Resource Center.)

The Surf beach house extended over the Gulf at Thirty-third Street. The exotic architecture featured tall towers and a Moorish decorative exterior. The Surf beach house opened in 1908 and was the site of the 1910 State Democratic Convention. Although it survived the 1909 hurricane, the 1915 hurricane damaged the structure beyond repair, and it was demolished shortly thereafter. (Courtesy of Center for 20th Century Texas Studies.)

This photograph is a close-up of the wooden ramps leading down to the water from the bathhouses. The picturesque quality of the image shows the beach full of tourists enjoying a variety of pastimes. (Courtesy of Galveston Historical Foundation's Preservation Resource Center.)

The automobile causeway constructed in 1911–1912 became an important lifeline to the mainland. Within a few years, automobile tourists would cross the causeway in anticipation of the island city. (Courtesy of DeGolyer Library, Southern Methodist, University, Dallas, Texas, Ag1982.0015.)

Under the auspices of the Moody family, the first Cotton Carnival in 1909 intended to bring tourists to Galveston to celebrate the role of cotton in the economy. The Port of Galveston was one of the world's largest centers of cotton shipping. Many of the local businesses sponsored floats in the parade, which were pulled by horses managed by an experienced horseman so they did not run rampant. The Cotton Carnival was short lived but included interesting parade floats such as this one with Egyptian figures. (Courtesy of Center for 20th Century Texas Studies.)

This 1910 panoramic photograph looks west from about Twenty-first Street and Seawall Boulevard. The protective iron fencing once along the sidewalk and top of the seawall is no longer visible, destroyed in the 1909 hurricane. The Boulevard Hotel and the Beach Hotel can be seen on the right, while the Seaside Hotel, the Electric Park, and Murdoch's Bathhouse can be seen in the distance. (Courtesy of Galveston Historical Foundation's Preservation Resource Center.)

Governor Colquitt opened the causeway in 1912 with 1,500 automobiles and an impressive ceremony. It would become the major point of access to the island. To the right of the automobile lanes is the rail line. (Courtesy of Dolph Briscoe Center for American History, University of Texas at Austin.)

The Galveston Flyer became the name of the interurban line from Houston to Galveston. This photograph shows passengers boarding on Twenty-first Street and Postoffice in Galveston. (Courtesy of Houston Metropolitan Research Center.)

The interurban provided transportation for businessmen but became an important way for tourists to access the island as well. This interior shot of the interurban captures the comfort and advertising of the day. (Courtesy of Houston Metropolitan Research Center.)

HOTEL GALVEZ
GALVESTON, TEXAS.

The Hotel Galvez opened in 1911 in an impressive ceremony signaling the new tourism commitment of the city. Throngs of cyclists, automobiles, and pedestrians converged on the front lawn. (Courtesy of DeGolyer Library, Southern Methodist University, Dallas, Texas, Ag2005.0001.)

Shortly after opening, the Hotel Galvez held a concert celebrating its architectural and economic achievement. This image shows the outdoor seating near the trolley tracks and parked automobiles. (Courtesy of Dolph Briscoe Center for American History, University of Texas at Austin.)

Within a few years, the open area to the west of the Hotel Galvez became the site of more amusements. The Orpheum Theater, a small Ferris wheel, and some tourist attractions made up the mix. (Courtesy of Dolph Briscoe Center for American History, University of Texas at Austin.)

A new carousel of extraordinary wooden horses made up the most popular attraction or ride. This rare photograph shows the beautifully crafted horses that were part of the Great American Derby ride. (Courtesy of Fred Huddleston, Private Collection.)

49

MILLION DOLLAR
HOTEL GALVEZ
ON SEAWALL BOULEVARD
GALVESTON, TEXAS

COPYRIGHTED BY
W. H. MORRIS

Pictured above is the highly trafficked seawall as crowds gathered in the 1910s outside Hotel Galvez. (Courtesy of Library of Congress.)

By 1915, Seawall Boulevard was an expansive street with a promenade along the water's edge. Handsome light standards illuminated the street at night and were an added attraction for tourists arriving in their automobiles. (Courtesy of Dolph Briscoe Center for American History, University of Texas at Austin.)

The 1915 hurricane destroyed much of the Electric Park and the attractive elements along Seawall Boulevard. In 1916, investors built the Crystal Palace with an impressive walkway over the street to the Gulf. To the left of the Palace, a large illuminated sign welcomes tourists at the end of Twenty-fifth Street. (Courtesy of Galveston County Museum.)

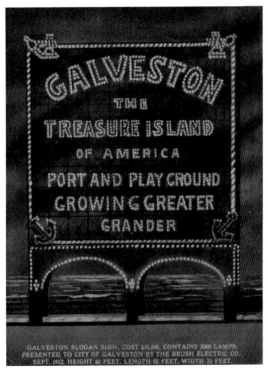

This large sign (above left) was a verbal welcome and advertisement for Galveston. It reflected the various names pinned on the island by tourist promoters in the early 20th century. "Treasure Island," "playground" and "growing, greater and grander" marked the promises made to each oncoming tourist. It was a gift to the city from the Brush Electric Company and contained 3,000 crimson and white lightbulbs. Above right, this candid photograph shows the fury of the 1919 hurricane and the subsequent demise of the large illuminated sign. (Left, courtesy of Galveston Historical Foundation's Preservation Resource Center; right, courtesy of Galveston County Museum.)

By 1920, the Crystal Palace was a major gathering place for tourists at the intersection of Twenty-fourth Street and Seawall Boulevard. An indoor saltwater swimming pool became one of the island's most popular spots. Taking the "plunge" included suspension wires over the water, a fountain, and lanes for swim meets. (Courtesy of Dolph Briscoe Center for American History, University of Texas at Austin.)

The Crystal Palace at night was just as fascinating as the former Electric Park. The ground-level arcades offered souvenirs, food, and games while the rooftop garden terrace provided a perfect spot for gazing over the Gulf waters or for watching the crowds of people below. During the bathing girl revues, spectators could pay a quarter for a bird's-eye view of the festivities from the roof of the Crystal Palace. (Courtesy of Center for 20th Century Texas Studies.)

This busy photograph of Murdoch's Bathhouse shows the first location for the 100-year-old Gaido's restaurant. Murdoch's, in a new form, post–Hurricane Ike, occupies the same location as the one in this photograph. (Courtesy of Galveston Historical Foundation's Preservation Resource Center.)

In 1911, San Jacinto Gaido opened his first café, a small seafood and steak restaurant, in the open-air rooms of Murdoch's Bathhouse. (Courtesy of Gaido's, Private Collection)

Andrew Fraser of Houston designed the Buccaneer Hotel for the Moody family in the late 1920s. The open arcade on the first floor catered to tourists while the upper rooms and banquet facilities heralded a new time of convention going. (Courtesy of Center for 20th Century Texas Studies.)

Looking east from Twenty-fifth Street on the seawall shows the juxtaposed Crystal Palace and Buccaneer Hotel. Murdoch's Bathhouse is on the right. (Courtesy of Galveston Historical Foundation's Preservation Resource Center.)

Galveston's more hedonistic days of the mid-20th century brought new attractions to the Gulf side of the seawall. The Grotto is a predecessor to the more famous Balinese Room. This rare photograph of the interior of the Grotto shows the imagery of the Asian-created decor. This photograph depicts the Pilot's Association Banquet, held there in 1935. (Courtesy of Dolph Briscoe Center for American History, University of Texas at Austin.)

The Balinese Room of the 1950s and 1960s was glamorous and sought to capture an exotic Asian feel. Operated by the Maceo family, it featured performers from around the United States and gambling in the back rooms. Gambling at the Balinese was a popular tourist activity until closed by the Texas Rangers in the 1950s. In 1961, Hurricane Carla brought major damage to the Balinese Room. The building and business was rebuilt and continued to operate before being completely destroyed by Hurricane Ike in 2008. (Courtesy of Galveston County Museum.)

Hurricane Carla also destroyed the Mountain Speedway roller coaster in 1961. Erected in 1921 and located behind the Buccaneer Hotel, the wooden roller coaster was several stories high. It was once surrounded by a small amusement park that included other amusement rides and concessions. (Courtesy of Galveston Historical Foundation's Preservation Resource Center.)

This photograph captures bathers between the Balinese Room and Murdoch's in the mid-20th century. In the background is a sign advertising the Turf Room, another gambling venue operated by the Maceo family. (Courtesy of Galveston Historical Foundation's Preservation Resource Center.)

Fresh Gulf seafood has always been an attraction on Galveston Island. The Seawall Café sat at Seventeenth Street and Seawall Boulevard and was best known for its catch-of-the-day offering. It advertised that patrons could bring in their catch of the day and the kitchen would prepare it any way patrons desired. (Courtesy of Galveston Historical Foundation's Preservation Resource Center.)

Gaido's restaurant is a local icon. In the 1940s, the restaurant moved its location at Seawall Boulevard and Thirty-ninth Street. The giant Gulf crab became a form of advertising for Gaido's in the 1970s. The iconic creature still rests on the roof of the restaurant today. (Courtesy of Gaido's, Private Collection.)

In September 2008, Hurricane Ike destroyed many Gulf venues. Today's Murdoch's replaces earlier buildings and continues the long tradition of the family business at its location on Seawall Boulevard and Twenty-third Street. (Photograph by David Canright.)

Galveston's beaches today are strewn with umbrellas and lounges just like earlier days. The beach remains the largest attraction for the island city. New events like sand castle building on East Beach are popular attractions for tourists. This early June event brings thousands to the island to participate or to admire the temporary works of art. (Courtesy of Galveston Island Convention and Visitors Bureau.)

The Seaside Hotel first appeared c. 1910 on the beach near Thirty-third Street. This popular hotel offered direct access to the beach and was within easy access of the trolley line. (Courtesy of Galveston Historical Foundation's Preservation Resource Center.)

The palatial and sprawling Mediterranean-style Hotel Galvez signaled the island's commitment to tourism that continues today. The hotel's towers are a landmark along the Gulf. The Hotel Galvez opened in 1911, introducing first-rate accommodations to the Gulf side of the island. Constructed at Twenty-first Street and Seawall Boulevard and designed by Mauran & Russell of St. Louis, Missouri, the Galvez could be reached by both trolley and automobile. (Courtesy of Tom Green, Private Collection.)

The Hotel Galvez faces the Gulf of Mexico, offering extensive walks and driveways on the water side. In its earliest days, hotel guests could rent wicker carts to cruise along the seawall. These rolling chairs were similar to those at Atlantic City, New Jersey, and were a popular way to enjoy the breezes and attractions. (Courtesy of Galveston Historical Foundation's Preservation Resource Center.)

The Seahorse Motel on Seawall Boulevard included a circular restaurant and office overlooking a pool. Built in 1956, Frances Moody and her sons contracted with Galveston architects Thomas Price and John Buckhart for this progressive modern design. (Courtesy of Tom Green, Private Collection.)

Hawkins Tourist Camp at Fourteenth Street and Seawall Boulevard illustrates a common development of tourist accommodations across the United States in the 1920s. Hawkins first opened a place for automobile campers, who often arrived with their own tent and rented a space. Sometimes called "tin can" tourists because they carried and ate food out of tin cans, this genre of tourist rather quickly began to seek sheltered accommodations. The Hawkins camp represents the private side of tourist accommodations while the City of Galveston offered free camping in a municipal park at Sixth-first Street. (Courtesy of Galveston Historical Foundation's Preservation Resource Center.)

Hawkins soon began to construct permanent small cottages that resembled domestic buildings of the 1920s (above left). Above right, the gas station and makeshift office for the cottages faced onto Seawall Boulevard at Fourteenth Street. Below left, the Gulf Terrace Hotel at 2527 Avenue Q sat near the seawall with rooms facing onto the Gulf. The Seawall Hotel included a popular café and apartments for long-term tourists (pictured below right). (Courtesy of Galveston Historical Foundation's Preservation Resource Center.)

The Cavalier Hotel is a modest example of hotels constructed in Galveston in the 1920s. While accessible by automobile, the hotel did not embrace the automobile in its design as others of the period did. The Cavalier was a hotel operated by the Moody family. (Courtesy of Center for 20th Century Texas Studies.)

In 1928, Andrew Fraser of Houston designed the Miramar Courts for the Moody family under Affiliated National Hotels. Located at 3402 Seawall Boulevard, Miramar quickly became the standard for an automobile-centered complex. This Spanish-influenced architecture was a complex of small rooms attached in rows set perpendicular to the seawall, gas stations, and eateries. The stucco exterior was similar to popular tourist courts across Texas that tried to mimic the state's indigenous architecture. (Courtesy of Center for 20th Century Texas Studies.)

The Affiliated National Hotels of the Moody family constructed the Edgewater Cabanas in 1933 on the beach at Seawall Boulevard and Sixth Street. The Edgewater was a colorful set of two-story gable-roofed huts flanked by a beach-like set of outdoor tables covered in palm leaves. The cabanas included a Shell gas station, food, and a camp office. The first floor of each hut had canvas shades that opened for breezes. (Courtesy of Center for 20th Century Texas Studies.)

The Affiliated National Hotels of the Moody family opened the Buccaneer Hotel in 1929. Designed by Houston architect Andrew Fraser, the multi-storied hotel dwarfed the grand Hotel Galvez one block away. The Buccaneer included banquet and convention facilities and an extensive arcade along Seawall Boulevard. (Courtesy of Center for 20th Century Texas Studies.)

Architect Andrew Fraser spared no money designing the interior of the Buccaneer Hotel. This photograph shows the heavy Spanish influence, including stenciled ceiling beams and extraordinary Batchelder tiles from California. The hotel was demolished on January 1, 1999. (Courtesy of Center for 20th Century Texas Studies.)

The Buccaneer Hotel sun deck is captured here in a rare photograph. It provided an unobstructed view of the Gulf of Mexico until it was demolished in 2000. (Courtesy of Center for 20th Century Texas Studies.)

In 1953, the Affiliated National Hotels owned by the Moody family built the Jack Tar Court Hotel at the end of Highway 75, the main north–south route through Texas. The Jack Tar boasted a fun theme that appealed to tourists until it was sold in 1973. The building was demolished in 1988. (Courtesy of Galveston Historical Foundation's Preservation Resource Center.)

The Jack Tar Court Hotel was a popular site for thousands of visitors to Galveston. It overlooked the Gulf of Mexico on East Beach Drive and Sixth Street. (Courtesy of Galveston Historical Foundation's Preservation Resource Center.)

Originally part of the Jack Tar hotel expansion completed in 1954, the Zig Zag Inn at Seventh and Beach Boulevard became an instant hit on East Beach. The creative architecture influenced the name "zig zag." (Courtesy of Tom Green, Private Collection.)

Designed by architects John J. Croft Jr. and H.S. Shannon, the Jack Tar (top) included a number of two-story buildings holding rooms, a café/restaurant, and one of the most attractive pools on the island. Thomas Price designed the Sandpiper (bottom) in 1963 for Dr. Edmond Henderson. This motel was on East Beach and provided direct access to the Gulf water. The motel was demolished in 2011. Today, the site is occupied by an upscale motor home resort. (Both, courtesy Tom Green, Private Collection)

The SS Galveston Hotel was a rare form of roadside architecture referred to as programmatic of mimetic, meaning mimicking something in order to draw attention. In 1941, Galveston architect Ben Milam designed the motel that appeared as an oceangoing vessel when viewed from Seawall Boulevard. It was demolished in 2006. (Courtesy of Galveston Historical Foundation's Preservation Resource Center.)

Gaido's Motor Hotel shows the bridge in terms between the older name "hotel" and the modern automobile oriented "motel." This complex was replaced by the current Gaido's Motel on Seawall Boulevard. (Courtesy Tom Green, Private Collection.)

The Hi Y camp (YMCA, above left) on the west end of the island is somewhat out of the ordinary for tourist accommodations. This photograph taken c. 1925 shows a modest complex for overnight stays, a pier for recreation, and a few boats used by guests. (Courtesy of Dolph Briscoe Center for American History, University of Texas at Austin.)

The Anchorage Motel (above left) opened in the 1960s on the corner of Seawall Boulevard and Twenty-seventh Street and represented the trend in modern design for tourist accommodations. This architect's rendering launched the first marketing efforts for the motel and shows how automobiles became integral to the design of the complex. Crockett Court (above right) overlooked the Gulf of Mexico with a slightly obstructed view by Fort Crockett between Forty-third and Forty-fifth Streets and Seawall Boulevard. The Crockett Court is one of the few complexes remaining from the 1930s. (Both, courtesy of Tom Green, Private Collection.)

George Mitchell built the San Luis hotel atop the World War II gunneries of Fort Crockett, seen here. Since 1984, the hotel has undergone a number of changes to become today's lavish resort complex. This 30-acre resort complex features world-class amenities, including a spa and conference center. (Courtesy of Galveston Historical Foundation's Preservation Resource Center.)

James E. Lyon, a Houston developer, contracted with the City of Galveston to reinvent the unprofitable Pleasure Pier with the Flagship Hotel. Designed by Neuhaus & Taylor of Houston with Thomas Price of Galveston, the Flagship boasted 240 luxury rooms in a seven-story box-like form. This modern hotel remained in operation until damaged by Hurricane Ike in September 2008. (Courtesy of Galveston Historical Foundation's Preservation Resource Center.)

This rare image, taken in 1941, shows the first stage of construction on the new Galveston Municipal Pleasure Pier. With the pier in place, construction of the buildings began in 1942. The new $1.5-million Galveston Municipal Pleasure Pier was completed in 1944. Because of delays caused by World War II, the pier was not fully opened until 1948. (Courtesy of Dolph Briscoe Center for American History, University of Texas at Austin.)

OPPOSITE: World War II caused intermittent delays in construction throughout the course of the Pleasure Pier project. This image, taken after August 1942, shows construction under way on the roof of the exhibit hall and the grandstands for the outdoor theater. (Courtesy of Dolph Briscoe Center for American History, University of Texas at Austin.)

THREE

THE PLEASURE PIER

The Pleasure Pier is one of the city's longest-lived ideas to boost island tourism. By 1912, Galveston's civic leaders imagined a pier similar to those in Atlantic City and Los Angeles. Though never developed, the idea stayed alive until 1931 when plans were drawn up for a 700-foot pier with an auditorium. Shortly before World War II, the city accepted a loan of $1.1 million from the federal government's Reconstruction Finance Corporation (RFC) and added another $350,000.

The pier became more popular in the 1950s when used for exhibits, conventions, and meetings. By 1957, the pier included rides, arcades, an aquarium, exhibit hall, the air-conditioned Marine Room ballroom, and fishing from the end of the pier. The outdoor theater featured diving exhibitions, concerts, theatrical performances, and motion pictures projected on a giant outdoor screen while the Marine Room drew premiere entertainers from all over the country. Each summer season, the official opening of the pier coincided with "Splash Day," one of the city's most famous tourist celebrations.

In 1957, the owners of the pier hired Howard Robbins as manager. He arrived from North Carolina with his family and lived on the pier for five years, in an apartment under the grandstands of the outdoor theater. In 1961, Hurricane Carla caused severe damage to the pier and amusements. Although a tourist destination for decades, the pier had never been profitable, and the city defaulted on the loan payments to the RFC.

In 1963, negotiations began between the city and Houston businessman James E. Lyon. Lyon purchased the defaulted bonds from the federal government and gave them to the city in exchange for $2 million in new bonds. The city immediately issued new bonds that were purchased by Lyon.

At the end of all the exchanges, Lyon built the Flagship Hotel, 240 luxury rooms that opened in 1965. He agreed to pay the city $185,000 a month in rent for 40 years, at the end of which the city would own both the hotel and the pier.

In 2005, Landry's Incorporated bought the long-neglected hotel from the city for $500,000. The hotel was already deteriorating when Hurricane Ike delivered the final blows in September 2008. Originally, Landry's reported it would consider restoring the hotel but after assessing the damage from Ike, the corporation made the announcement in October 2010 that it planned to demolish the hotel and return the pier to its roots as an amusement facility.

Demolition began in February 2011 and was completed by June. By January 2012, the multimillion-dollar restoration was under way. The new Historic Pleasure Pier opened in June 2012. The approximately 1,130-foot pier extends over the Gulf of Mexico and features a first-class, nostalgically themed amusement park reminiscent of another historic landmark, Galveston's Electric Park.

This image, taken on May 18, 1943, shows the exterior buildings completed. During this period, the US Army and Navy had requisitioned the pier for storage space. Construction began shortly before World War II began. The war interrupted construction on the pier until 1944 and its opening until 1948. Designed by Galveston architect Raymond Rapp, the Galveston Municipal Pleasure Pier consisted of a four-block-long pier featuring a collection of modest streamlined buildings and structures, including a ballroom, 2,000-seat outdoor theater, open-air aquarium, snack bar, fishing from the T-head at the back of the pier, and other concessions. The pier proved less popular than civic leaders had anticipated, partially because so little of its enclosed space was open to the cool Gulf breezes. In 1947, the city leased the pier to Galveston businessmen W.L. Moody Jr., Herbert S. Autrey, and the Maceo family's business interest. The new owners formed the Galveston Pier Corporation, and in June, secretary Richard Klaerner announced that the pier would be partially opened that season. The exhibit hall and auditorium would remain closed as new air-conditioning units were being installed. (Courtesy of Dolph Briscoe Center for American History, University of Texas at Austin.)

By 1957, the new owners had air-conditioned the interior exhibit hall and ballroom while carnival rides had been added to the front of the pier. (Courtesy of Howard Robbins family, Private Collection.)

Pleasure Pier management invested $250,000 in upgrades for the pier in 1957. In addition to the rides and attractions, an elaborate lighting system was also added. Howard Robbins (second from right) was hired to manage the pier that same year. (Courtesy of Howard Robbins family, Private Collection.)

The opening of the Pleasure Pier coincided with Splash Day, a four-day event featuring parades, concerts, and a beauty contest. In this 1957 photograph, contestants in the Miss Splash Day contest can be seen with the event promoters, posing at the entrance to the Pleasure Pier. More than 300 young women entered the beauty contest that year. Pat Wells, an 18-year-old high school senior from Pasadena, Texas, was named Miss Splash Day. (Courtesy of Howard Robbins family, Private Collection.)

People gather around the entrance of the Pleasure Pier in anticipation of the 1957 Splash Day parade. (Courtesy of Howard Robbins family, Private Collection.)

Beachgoers scramble to catch one of the 300 cork balls being dropped from a helicopter during the Pleasure Pier opening day festivities in 1957. The numbered balls were redeemable at the Pleasure Pier for prizes. (Courtesy of Howard Robbins family, Private Collection.)

The pier's Ferris wheel and merry-go-round are shown in this image. Located on the right side of the pier, the rides were part of the upgrades initiated in 1957. (Courtesy of Howard Robbins family, Private Collection.)

The north end of the Pleasure Pier featured rides for small children. A temporary sign over the Amusement Hall door announces a "free Coca Cola" party for kids on Saturday, August 17. (Courtesy of Howard Robbins family, Private Collection.)

The Marine Room ballroom was located inside the Amusement Hall. Air-conditioned by 1948, the massive room was available for private parties as well as public events hosted by the pier's management. (Courtesy of Howard Robbins family, Private Collection.)

Mel Arvin, leader of the Mel Arvin Orchestra, was a frequent performer at the Marine Room. Hailed as the "best dance band in the Southwest" by local newspapers, Arvin and his orchestra were renowned for having played in clubs and hotels throughout the country, including the Dixie Club in Manhattan and various show bars in Las Vegas. The Mel Arvin Orchestra also performed at the Balinese Room during the 1960s. (Courtesy of Jami Durham, Private Collection.)

The Marine Room attracted entertainers from all over the United States. In this image, dancers enjoy the swinging sounds of the Buddy Brock Orchestra, led by Houstonian Clarence L. "Buddy" Brock Jr. (Courtesy of Howard Robbins family, Private Collection.)

Jazz musician, clarinetist, and big band leader Woody Herman was also a popular headliner at the Marine Room. His orchestra, known as the "Thundering Herd," toured the United States as well as Europe. In 1963, Herman was awarded a Grammy for his jazz album *Encore* and a second Grammy in 1973 for his big band jazz album *Giant Steps*. After his death in 1987, Herman was awarded the Grammy Lifetime Achievement Award. (Courtesy of Howard Robbins family, Private Collection.)

In 1957, the Walker Dick Water Show was featured daily at the outdoor theater at the back of the Pleasure Pier. A diving and acrobatic exhibition, the 2,000-seat grandstand was always full when entertainers took the stage. (Courtesy of Howard Robbins family, Private Collection.)

One of the most breathtaking acts was performed by Larry Ruhl and Sandy Winters. Both world-famous acrobats, the two amazed spectators with their helicopter act, shown here. After diving from the 112-foot platform, Ruhl would hang from the helicopter as he lifted Winters back up to the top of the platform via a rope and ring. (Courtesy of Howard Robbins family, Private Collection.)

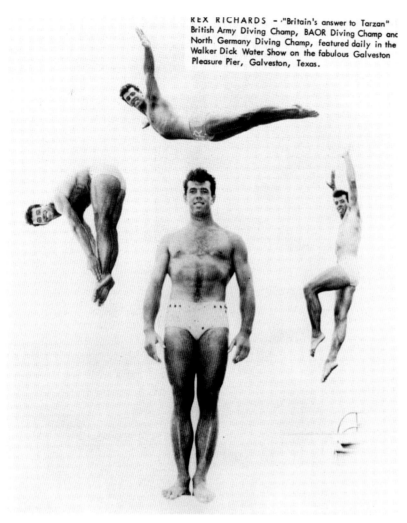

REX RICHARDS - "Britain's answer to Tarzan" British Army Diving Champ, BAOR Diving Champ and North Germany Diving Champ, featured daily in the Walker Dick Water Show on the fabulous Galveston Pleasure Pier, Galveston, Texas.

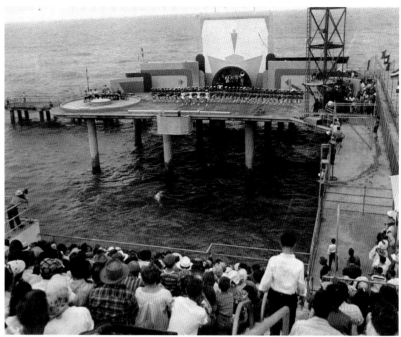

The Kilgore Rangerettes led the five-mile opening Splash Day parade in 1958, kicking off four days of activities and performances. They are seen here performing in May 1958 at the outdoor theater on the back of the pier. (Courtesy of Howard Robbins family, Private Collection.)

In June, 1957, the *Galveston Daily News* heralded the arrival of the "Tarzan of the Diving Board," Rex Richards. A British army diving champion, Richards headlined the water circus during the summer of 1957. (Courtesy of Howard Robbins family, Private Collection.)

This 1957 image shows friends after a successful day of fishing. From left to right are Mr. and Mrs. Ernest Neff and Maggie Bryan of Dallas and Mrs. and Mr. Albert Lewis Jr. of Galveston posing proudly with their stringer of fish. (Courtesy of Howard Robbins family, Private Collection.)

The T-head at the back of the Pleasure Pier was always a popular fishing spot. Anglers were almost always guaranteed a catch. This image shows an unidentified fisherman with his catch of the day. (Courtesy of Howard Robbins family, Private Collection.)

The Pleasure Pier is seen here at dusk in 1957. (Courtesy of Howard Robbins family, Private Collection.)

Underneath the neon Coca-Cola sign was the Pleasure Pier Diner and the Treasure Chest Souvenir and Gift Shop, shown in this evening image taken c. 1960. (Courtesy of Howard Robbins family, Private Collection.)

In September 1961, Hurricane Carla arrived, ending the Pleasure Pier's reign as a waterfront tourist destination. (Courtesy of Galveston County Museum.)

In 1965, Houston financier James Lyon opened the Flagship Hotel, which included luxury rooms, a restaurant and bar, and an elevated swimming pool. Fishing resumed at the back of the pier, with a small building added for concessions. Hurricane Ike damaged the hotel beyond repair in 2008. The structure was demolished in 2011. Because of environmental concerns, netting was erected around the base of the pier and the hotel was demolished one floor at a time, starting at the top. (Courtesy of Galveston Historical Foundation's Preservation Resource Center.)

Opened in May 2012, the new Historic Pleasure Pier bridges Galveston's past with the present, resurrecting the waterfront attraction. (Photograph by David Canright; courtesy of Galveston Historical Foundation's Preservation Resource Center.)

Today's Pleasure Pier features family-oriented attractions with 16 rides, midway games, retail shops, and a wide selection of food venues, including Texas's first Bubba Gump Shrimp Co. (Photograph by David Canright; courtesy of Galveston Historical Foundation's Preservation Resource Center.)

Galvestonians made use of the varied fishing venues, from the bay to the Gulf, jetties, and fishing vessels. This photograph shows a popular way for the sportsman to display his catch of the day. (Courtesy of Galveston Historical Foundation's Preservation Resource Center.)

OPPOSITE: This early-20th-century image of the Twenty-first Street fishing pier shows the concession area and partially covered T-head at the back of the pier. (Courtesy of Dolph Briscoe Center for American History, University of Texas at Austin.)

SPORTS AND RECREATION

Galveston Island is an outdoor paradise for many sports and forms of recreation. Early in the community's history, fishing became a favorite pastime on the bay, in the bayous set into the island, and later in the Gulf of Mexico. Galvestonians used small rowboats on the island lakes and in the bay but larger excursion vessels became a popular way to see the island and local highlights. The excursion vessels were both privately owned and available for charter, attracting groups for pleasure trips. In time, these folded into a combination of pleasure boating, yachting, and large-scale fishing ventures. Other water-based sports soon appeared on the island, including competitive sailing and row clubs.

Other sports also found use on the island. The sport of boxing found an easy start on the docks of Galveston. Jack Johnson became one of the nation's greatest pugilists, but others also gained their footing on the island.

The state's first baseball games originated here, organized by Gen. Abner Doubleday, near the former St. Mary's Infirmary on the east end. Doubleday, associated with the beginnings of baseball in the United States, had arrived in Galveston on November 4, 1866, as commander of the Army's forces here following the Civil War. In short time, Doubleday became the assistant commissioner of the Freedman's Bureau, where he stayed until August 1, 1867. Doubleday formed the Galveston Base Ball Club in January 1867 and drew out the first baseball diamond in Texas in front of the city hospital on the east end of the island. The Houston Stonewalls played the Galveston Robert E. Lees with the Stonewalls winning 35-2. The local interest in baseball eventually developed into a number of local teams forming.

Founders of the Galveston Golf and Country

Club introduced the sport of golfing on the island and built the state's first golf course. Hunting fowl and other game flourished on the west end as cooler months became ideal hunting times for migrating birds. Auto racing on the beach became one of the most interesting sporting activities. The hard-packed sand was ideal for the early automobile enthusiasts who quickly set up races.

Surfing began in the Hawaiian Islands when Polynesians discovered that the abundant surf made for a challenging sport as well as recreation. By the early 20th century, surfing fell out of popularity and few knew what it was, even in Hawaii. The water sport revived in post–World War II years as Hawaii became a destination for thousands of Americans. The newest state in the union introduced tourists to the age-old tradition of surfing and inspired others to take it to the mainland. Southern California in the 1950s offered surfing teams, tournaments, and a new subculture of young men and women who congregated on the beaches to surf the waves on long boards. These surfboards were often massive and heavy but suitable for the large waves of Hawaii and Southern California. The newly revived sport spawned movies like *Gidget*, and music like that of the Beach Boys added to the subculture.

The Gulf Coast communities found few surfers until the mid-1960s, probably because the large surfboards did not function well along the Gulf Coast. In July 1963, Cecil Laws of Corpus Christi began renting surfboards in Galveston, on the beach in front of Gaido's restaurant. Laws had traveled to Hawaii with his family and observed surfing in the islands. He returned and began renting surfboards on Padre Island. A year later he brought the business to Galveston.

Within a few years, young surfers gathered on Galveston Island for tournaments and daily recreation. Surf shops opened and the seawall swelled with automobiles of the surfers. Several places along the seawall became popular especially at the Thirty-seventh Street fishing pier and on the west side of the Flagship Hotel. In 1964, the Galveston City Council passed an ordinance restricting the locations for surfing at the insistence of a few business owners along the seawall. The "surfniks," as some described them, continued to increase in number despite the concerns of some Galvestonians. Surfing developed nationally into a respectable sport, and winners of the Galveston competitions went on to Huntington Beach, California, for the National Surfing Championships.

The Galveston waters were home to many species of fish and other sea creatures. Catching a large fish always caught the eye of visitors and photographers. (Courtesy of Dolph Briscoe Center for American History, University of Texas at Austin.)

Capt. R.L. Bettison operated one of the most popular fishing accommodations in the city. His pier and fishing house were seven miles from the city on the North Jetty. Bettison offered transportation to the fishing pier, by way of a launch, from his office at Pier 19. This is still the location for many private fishing charter companies. (DeGolyer Library, Southern Methodist, University, Dallas, Texas, Ag2009.0005)

The fishing pier featured places to purchase bait and fishing tackle, sleeping accommodations for men, and a European café. Advertised as the "deep blue waters of the Gulf," mackerel and tarpon were an easy catch. (Courtesy of Galveston Historical Foundation's Preservation Resource Center.)

Go Fishing—Bettison's Fishing Pier Co.
Galveston, Texas
In the Deep Blue Waters of the Gulf

Mackerel
Tarpon

On North Jetty, Seven Miles from City.

Launches make regular trips daily. Leave Chapman's Wharf, Pier 19, at 5:30 and 9:30 a. m. and 1:30 and 5:30 p.m. Returning leave Fishing Pier one hour later Extra trips as required.

Meals, Bait and Fishing Tackle can be secured at Pier. Telephone 59. Sleeping accommodations for men. W. J. Chapman, Gen. Manager.

The North Jetty lay across from the South Jetty and included lifesaving facilities and, at various times, quarantine accommodations. The jetty is a rough set of granite boulders still visible and used today. (Courtesy of Galveston Historical Foundation's Preservation Resource Center.)

Bettison's pier allowed for family outings where children and domestic help joined in catching the fish. The pier was destroyed in the 1909 hurricane. (Courtesy of Galveston Historical Foundation's Preservation Resource Center.)

The Tarpon Fishing Pier opened in May 1909. Six miles from the city on the North Jetty, it included accommodations for men and women and a first-class café. Its existence, however, was short lived as it was destroyed in the 1909 hurricane as well. Captain Bettison and his wife as well as other guests were killed in the hurricane. (Courtesy of Center for 20th Century Texas Studies.)

The Galveston Golf and Country Club formed in the 1890s and would boast the largest membership of any similar organization in Galveston. The club built its first clubhouse and 18-hole seaside golf course in the Denver Resurvey area. Club members introduced the sport of golfing to the island and hosted tournaments and invited nationally known golfers to play on the course. (Courtesy of Galveston County Museum.)

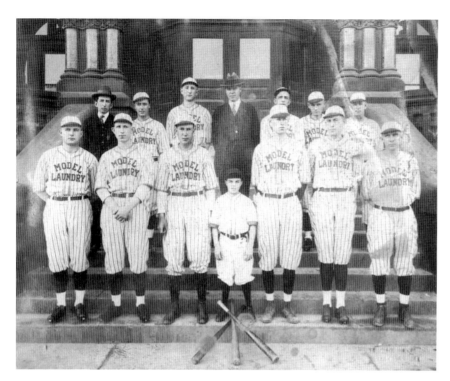

Abner Doubleday set up the first baseball game in Texas for February 22, 1867, with the first intercity match held on Texas Independence Day, April 21, 1867. In the early 20th century, Galvestonians organized a city league made up of teams from local businesses, including the Model Laundry housed a Twenty-fifth and Church Streets. (Courtesy of Galveston Historical Foundation's Preservation Resource Center.)

Clarke & Courts printing on Mechanic and Twenty-fourth Streets supported another team that played in a city league. Baseball became an ever-popular sport in the first half of the 20th century. (Courtesy of Galveston County Museum.)

The Galveston Sand Crabs baseball team formed in 1906 to play in the Texas League. This statewide league (and slightly beyond because it at one time included Oklahoma and Louisiana) operated through the 1920s. Galveston's diamond became known as the "little cigar box" that looked like a turtle when covered with tarps for rain protection. The diminutive size of the diamond allegedly made it easier to make home runs. (Courtesy of Galveston County Museum.)

The Cascade team represented a second laundry on Galveston Island. These city commercial teams set up a lively league schedule throughout the spring months. (Courtesy of Galveston Historical Foundation's Preservation Resource Center.)

In 1910, Johnson appeared for a week at New York City's Hammerstein's Theatre on Forty-second Street. This image shows a large crowd waiting to see the "Galveston Giant." Johnson lost the title in 1915. He continued to fight professionally until 1938. (Courtesy of the Library of Congress.)

Boxing was an early sport in Galveston with its presumed beginnings among the longshoremen working the docks. While evidence suggests that the laboring men partook of fighting in the 19th century, African American laborers appeared to be among the first to engage in a semiprofessional sport. Kid Gardner of Galveston challenged others in New Orleans in 1905 and in 1906, beginning a series of wins. Jack Johnson, born in Galveston in 1878, however, may be among the most significant boxers in the United States. He broke the color lines with his winning of the World Heavyweight Championship in 1908. (Courtesy of Library of Congress.)

The Galveston Rowing Club formed in September 1873 at the armory of the Lone Star Rifles on Tremont Street. The newspaper announced that rowing clubs were taking the place of baseball clubs in many cities, including New Orleans. The club set out to purchase boats and find a boathouse that was later set up on Kuhn's Wharf. The Galveston Rowing Club sponsored its first regatta with the Bay Yacht Club in August 1874. The rowing club included classes for four and six oarsmen. In 1880, a second rowing club formed with just 30 members. Named the Protection Rowing Club, their membership had more than tripled by 1882. (Courtesy of Galveston County Museum.)

The Bay Yacht Club existed as early as 1874, offering joint races with the Galveston Rowing Club. In July 1893, the Galveston Corinthian Yacht Club sponsored a regatta, and then in 1895, the Galveston Yacht Club formed and began its own regatta. The Galveston Boat and Yacht Club reorganized in 1903 and erected its first permanent boathouse on Pelican Island in c. 1906. (Courtesy of Galveston County Museum.)

Visible from the end of Tremont Street where the club maintained a private launch, the handsome Craftsman-inspired clubhouse with twin towers sat on five acres. The building included accommodations, reading rooms, gaming spaces, a ballroom, and wooden walkways with spacious decks. The club owned powerboats, single and double shells, and a host of smaller racing shells. (Courtesy of Galveston County Museum.)

Yachting was already a popular aquatic sport in the Northeast, and newspapers often referred to the natural water setting of Galveston as ideal for the sport in the island city. (Courtesy of Galveston County Museum.)

In celebration of the 89th anniversary of the Battle of San Jacinto, the boat and yacht club hosted "power" boat races in the harbor on April 21, 1925. Newspapers announced the closing of banks and schools for the holiday, and the excursion boat *Galvez* offered trips to the battleground, located 40 miles north on Crystal Bay. (Courtesy of Dolph Briscoe Center for American History, University of Texas at Austin.)

The Galveston Yacht Club initiated a plan to purchase property at the end of the seawall at Sixth Street on the bay side in the 1920s. The full marina as it is known today was mostly constructed in the 1950s as the east end of Galveston developed. (Courtesy of Galveston Historical Foundation's Preservation Resource Center.)

The *Mariner* was an early steam-powered excursion boat owned by local businessmen Charles T. Sunderman and Ben Dolson Jr. Travel even for a short time on the *Mariner* would have been noisy and dirty but with more speed and a shorter travel time, a popular venture. (Courtesy of Galveston Historical Foundation's Preservation Resource Center.)

The Lakewood Yacht Club sponsors the annual Harvest Mood Regatta that leaves Galveston for Port Aransas each year in October. This event fills the Gulf of Mexico at the end of the pier at Twenty-fifth Street with boats of all shapes and sizes. (Galveston Island Convention and Visitors Bureau.)

The *Colonel Galveston* was a smaller excursion boat that offered transportation and adventure in the early 20th century. None of the early excursion boats remain in use in Galveston. (Courtesy of Galveston Historical Foundation's Preservation Resource Center.)

The Galveston Bowling Association formed in the late 19th century but reformed in 1909. Bowling became the island's most popular sport by the sheer numbers of participation. Introduced by German immigrants to the island, the German social club Garten Verein had the first bowling alley in Galveston. The German style of bowling originated at festivals where socializing and a good time were more important than athletic abilities. (Courtesy of Galveston Historical Foundation's Preservation Resource Center.)

Shortly after the formation of the Galveston Automobile Club, local automobile owners introduced racing on the beach. On November 29, 1906, the automobile club sponsored its first race. An estimated 3,000 people watched as the competing automobiles completed five races. The beach area utilized was seldom touched by water and included many "lumps" that slowed the drivers. (Courtesy of Galveston Historical Foundation's Preservation Resource Center.)

In 1921, the Dusenberg Racing Team participated, led by Eddie Rickenbacker, a World War I flying ace and later head of Eastern Airlines. Automobile racing was a harrowing sport in those days, as recorded by Rickenbacker biographer W. David Lewis: "In a 300-mile race at Galveston, Texas, one of his tires blew out when he was going 90 miles an hour. Instead of coming off the rim, it got caught and flapped repeatedly across his left arm and shoulder, hitting him like a club." Eddie O'Donnell climbed from his seat where he was riding and threw his body across Rickenbacker's, absorbing the blows. O'Donnell is pictured here, on the left, seated beside Rickenbacker, who is behind the wheel. (Courtesy of Auburn University Libraries Special Collections and Archives Department.)

The races became a popular event held during the Cotton Carnival each spring. The 1925 Cotton Carnival races occurred in front of bleachers erected for the race each year. These temporary stands collapsed during the 1913 races, injuring a number of spectators. These races grew in popularity until discontinued about 1930. (Courtesy of Galveston Historical Foundation's Preservation Resource Center.)

The Galveston Kennel and Fair Association brought greyhound racing to Galveston in 1927. From July through September that year, spectators watched the dogs compete by chasing an electric rabbit. The track grandstands accommodated 4,000 people and included a refreshment stand on the ground floor and a dance floor in the rooftop salon. Opening night drew over 7,500 spectators with city streetcars running to the track every 10 minutes. Despite the successful summer, the races were not repeated in 1928. Horse racing was an early sport on the island beginning as early as the 1840s. In 1933, Houston businessman Bassett Blakely signed a five-year lease on the abandoned dog track and opened Galveston Downs, bringing thoroughbred horse racing to Galveston. The grandstands were improved and a modern half-mile track was added, along with adequate stables for the thoroughbreds and outbuildings to house equipment, the jockeys, and permanent concession stands. (Both, courtesy of Galveston Historical Foundation's Preservation Resource Center.)

GALVEZ HOTEL, SEAWALL & BEACH
GALVESTON, TEX.

Originally named aeroplanes, these aircraft were part of the first aviation meet Galveston hosted in February 1912. Pilots buzzed the beachfront and seawall to gain attention. The meet was held at the aviation park located in the Denver Resurvey at Fifty-third Street and Avenue R. (Courtesy of Tom Green, Private Collection.)

The first meet featured famed aviator Charles Hamilton (1885–1914), who flew his 60-horsepower Curtiss biplane into Galveston for the first time. The most remarkable part of Hamilton's visit was his race along the beach with an automobile, captured by Galveston photographer H.H. Morris. (Courtesy of Galveston Historical Foundation's Preservation Resource Center.)

Pictured here is a close-up of Hamilton in his biplane. Other aviators at the Galveston meet also completed notable stunts, like landing on the seawall. (Courtesy of the Library of Congress.)

By the 1960s, surfers were catching waves between the jetties near the foot of Thirty-third Street. Hill's Seafood Restaurant and the Seahorse Motel can be seen in the background. The Gulf Coast communities found few surfers until the mid-1960s, probably because traditionally large surfboards did not function well along the Gulf Coast. In July 1963, Cecil Laws of Corpus Christi began renting surfboards in Galveston, on the beach in front of Gaido's restaurant. Within a few years, young surfers gathered on Galveston Island for tournaments and daily recreation. Surf shops opened and the seawall swelled with automobiles of the surfers. Several places along the seawall became popular, especially at the Thirty-seventh Street fishing pier and on the west side of the Flagship Hotel. In 1964, the Galveston City Council passed an ordinance restricting the locations for surfing at the insistence of a few business owners along the seawall. The "surfniks," as some described them, continued to increase in number despite the concerns of some Galvestonians. (Courtesy of Bob Morris, Private Collection.)

Surfing developed nationally into a respectable sport, and winners of the Galveston competitions went on to Huntington Beach, California, for the National Surfing Championships. Surf shops literally sprang up in Galveston by 1965. Most shops opened along the seawall in small buildings or houses. Ken's Surf Shop, located at Seawall Boulevard and Twenty-seventh Street rented surfboards from their temporary shops set up on the beach. (Courtesy of Bob Morris, Private Collection.)

The surfboard has changed dramatically since the inception of the sport. The Hawaiians used wooden planks of redwood, mahogany, and balsa wood weighing as much as 150 pounds, but by the 1960s, boards measured eight, nine, or 10 feet in length and were made of plastic or fiberglass. The chemical industry contributed significantly to the new materials, making plastics affordable and plentiful. These new boards frequently weighed about 30 pounds (sometimes up to 50 pounds) and came in a variety of colors and forms. The new lighter weight surfboards were suitable for the smaller Gulf waves found in Galveston. (Courtesy of Bob Morris, Private Collection.)

The Galveston Chapter, Order of DeMolay hosted the first surfing competitions in Galveston. In 1965, Bert Thompson and Clifford Searcy cochaired the event using Ken's Surf Shop at 2120 Twenty-seventh Street as the contest headquarters. In September of the following year, the DeMolays held their second contest at the Thirty-seventh Street surf area with 82 participants from the Galveston and Houston area. Surfing captured the attention of *Texas Parade Magazine*; the August 1965 publication showed surfers east of the new Flagship Hotel. The magazine noted that the guests of the Flagship had a special view of the surfers. (Courtesy of Bob Morris, Private Collection.)

The Dewey Weber Company of Venice, California, sponsored its own surfing contest in July 1966. While meant for local surfers, the Weber Company sought to develop a national following for surfing and to introduce the Gulf Coast to surfing magazines. (Courtesy of Bob Morris, Private Collection.)

The Pepsi Texas State Surfing Championship attracted an ever larger crowd of spectators and participants. In 1969, the third championship hosted 15,000 spectators and almost 350 entrants. (Courtesy of Bob Morris, Private Collection.)

Galveston has long promoted its beaches for tourists, but surfing brought a whole new look and age to the island. The typical Memorial Day-to-Labor Day tourist season proved a challenge to island businesses that wanted an extended season. Oddly, surfers defied the limits of the holidays and became a much more reliable visitor earlier in the year, usually by April and well past September. (Courtesy of Bob Morris, Private Collection.)

The Fifth Annual Pepsi State Surfing Championship continued to attract large crowds in April 1971. The organizers expected 400 surfers. Participants had to be Texas residents for six months to enter and found their entry forms on Pepsi cartons. (Courtesy of Bob Morris, Private Collection.)

In the sixth year, the event renamed itself to the Pepsi-KAUM Texas State Surfing Championship and attracted its largest crowds. The event coincided with the Shrimp Festival and sand castle–building competition in an effort to invite visitors to Galveston. (Courtesy of Bob Morris, Private Collection.)

In 1973, Galveston College boasted its own surfing team and won first place in the competition among Gulf Coast surfers. Tom Jones, captain of the team, combined his surfing interests with photography. Surfers still flock to Galveston today. They can mainly be seen west of the Pleasure Pier and east of the Thirty-seventh Street jetty. (Courtesy of Bob Morris, Private Collection.)

This set of beach beauties, both male and female, show swimwear of 1918. The beach also allowed the subject of photographers to pose in creative ways. (Courtesy of Fred Huddleston, Private Collection.)

Socially acceptable bathing wear in the late 19th and early 20th century changed dramatically within a few decades. This group of Galveston beachgoers posed at Louis Tobler's photography studio at Murdoch's Bathhouse in what might be called conservative beachwear. (Courtesy of Galveston Historical Foundation's Preservation Resource Center.)

OPPOSITE: Another set of beach beauties poses under Murdoch's near a granite boulder. The dark wool suits with bathing caps seemed anything but alluring. (Courtesy of Fred Huddleston, Private Collection.)

FIVE

BATHING BEAUTIES

Galvestonians began to recognize the tourism value of the Gulf of Mexico in the early 20th century. As elaborate beachfront buildings appeared along the south side of the island facing the Gulf waters, local businessmen conceived of special events that would draw tourists to the new attractions and the island in general. One of the most important special events came from the efforts of the Galveston Beach Association.

The Galveston Beach Association formed early in the 20th century to promote tourism through events offered on an annual basis. The first of its many efforts was Splash Day in May of each year, serving as the opening of the summer tourist season. In a seemingly unlikely and unfamiliar special event, the association organized the first Bathing Girl Revue in 1916 as an activity to build on the natural beach setting and appeal to a large number of visitors. Described as a beauty pageant, young women competed from communities around the nation and later, the world, in bathing attire and evening dresses.

The earliest photographs indicate that a costume sometimes of exaggerated proportions served as bathing attire. In the first two to three years, contestants devised costumes of bright colors, often ill fitted, and sought an appeal that was other than simply beauty. As the Bathing Girl Revue increased in popularity, the revue welcomed changes, including altering the name to the International Pageant of Pulchritude in 1926 that bestowed a title of Miss Universe on the winner. Both the title of Bathing Girl Revue

and International Pageant of Pulchritude were used for the event from 1926 to 1931. Personal accounts of the revue describe a number of days that constituted the event leading up to the final competition.

In later years, American contestants competed first for the Miss USA title and then the Miss Universe award. Although not directly connected to the current Miss Universe pageant, the concept of an international competition to identify a beautiful young woman with talent was established in Galveston. Other coastal communities, including Atlantic City, New Jersey, and Long Beach, California, also offered beauty pageants but without the appeal of the Galveston event.

The beauty pageants attracted large crowds, particularly young men, and involved intense preparations on the part of Galvestonians. Banquets, private teas, and scores of newspaper stories extolling the characteristics of various participants made for a festive week comparable to Mardi Gras in New Orleans. The winners of the pageant received a cash prize as well as other items and became an instant celebrity in her own community. Dorothy Britton of New York won the coveted title in 1927 and would be photographed across the country as she returned home by train. Several prizewinning women became performers in vaudeville shows and in the emerging motion picture industry.

The International Pageant of Pulchritude ceased in 1931, a victim of the Great Depression and possibly a less-accepting social climate. The competition moved to Brussels, Belgium, for two years and then ended. In 1952, the Miss Universe pageant of modern times began in California. Another bathing beach revue returned to the island in 2009 under the sponsorship of the group Islander By Choice, LLC.

By 1920 (the second year of the event), the Bathing Girl Revue attracted 20,000 spectators. Bathing attire, or at least that seen in this competition, had changed dramatically. These three prizewinners posed on the sand in what appears more like a costume. Alma Ralston, in the center of the photograph, won the most original costume with patches and a hoop skirt. Bonnie Bremer, right, of Houston won "most becoming" in a royal purple costume. (Courtesy of Galveston Historical Foundation's Preservation Resource Center.)

Some of the 1920 participants staged themselves on the granite boulders across the street from the Crystal Palace where the competition was held. Reba Dick of Galveston won the grand prize and is in the upper left of the photograph. Dick wore a scarlet costume with a red silk accordion cape and ribbon bathing cap. (Courtesy of Galveston Historical Foundation's Preservation Resource Center.)

This bathing beauty of the early 1920s stood on the granite boulders of the Gulf of Mexico holding a parasol. Her bathing attire shows a major shift from covering all of the body to reducing the covered portions to the main parts of the anatomy. (Courtesy of Houston Metropolitan Research Center.)

Local publisher Clarke & Courts issued an interesting set of stamps in the 1910s. This stamp featured an early bathing beauty wringing her skirt after swimming in the Gulf. (Courtesy of Galveston Historical Foundation's Preservation Resource Center.)

The Bathing Beauty Revue (top) included 108 entries on May 14, 1922. An estimated 100,000 attended to watch the parade from Thirteenth Street to Menard Park and then to Crystal Palace. Pauline Hampton of Dallas was the grand-prize winner. The pageant participants designed elaborate costumes rather than just emphasizing form and style. In May 1923, the revue seems to have had fewer participants (bottom). Despite that, Galveston spent $40,000 in advertising and closed streets to traffic. Mary Wilmot of Houston won the grand prize of $500. Most artistic costume went to Effie Ludwig of Houston. (Both, courtesy of Library of Congress.)

This small group of 1923 contestants illustrates the diversity of ideas in costuming. Bathing caps were especially artful along with stockings and heels. (Courtesy of Galveston Historical Foundation's Preservation Resource Center.)

This photograph of the Bathing Girl Revue captured the crowds that lined the parade route on Seawall Boulevard. The crowd sat along the seawall itself to view the competition for the first time in 1925. More than 20,000 people arrive by automobile, and others came in eight special trains from Houston. Miss Chicago won the grand prize in 1925. (Courtesy of Galveston County Museum.)

In 1926, promoters changed the name of the competition to the First International Pageant of Pulchritude (top). A $2,000 prize went to Catherine Moylan of Dallas for first place. That year the event included international participants and the emphasis on form, figure, and beauty seemed to clearly rate over costume. In May 1927, Galveston sponsored the Second International Pageant of Pulchritude, or the Eighth Bathing Beauty Revue (bottom). Five foreign representatives (Italy, France, Luxembourg, Portugal, and Cuba) participated and arrived on the French liner *Niagara* on May 1. (Courtesy of Library of Congress.)

The late-1920s pageants included fewer participants but a much more glamorous group. Taking the official photograph of the contestants lined up on the beach after the competition became yet another event for the spectators to enjoy. (Courtesy of Houston Metropolitan Research Center.)

The 1927 pageant welcomed more than 250,000 spectators at the city auditorium. The winner, Dorothy Britton of New York, is captured here by a photographer in Chicago as she was returning home. (Courtesy of Chicago History Museum.)

One of the thrilling moments for contestants was the parade along Seawall Boulevard near Twenty-fifth Street. The crowd included large groups of young men and a few stylish women. Contestants stood in the back seat of handsome automobiles often supported by a pole attached to a viewing box. Spectators could get within a few feet of the automobiles. (Courtesy of Karen Glazener Kremer, Private Collection.)

This striking photograph shows a large crowd positioned on the seawall to watch the competition. In the background, the Hotel Galvez looms over the amusement park next to it. The seawall at this location was a popular place for community events. (Courtesy of Fred Huddleston, Private Collection.)

Fifth International Pageant of Pulc.
Galvest

The Third International Pageant of Pulchritude and Ninth Bathing Beauty Revue (top) occurred in June 1928. There were two competitions included, one for Miss United States and a second for Miss Universe. Ella Van Hueson of Chicago represented the United States and then went on to win Miss Universe. In August 1930, Galveston hosted the Fifth International Pageant of Pulchritude (bottom). Dorothy Dell Goff of New Orleans won Miss United States and went on to be Miss Universe. She was crowned at the Buccaneer Hotel on Seawall Boulevard. This photograph shows the maturity of the competition to include evening dresses as well as swimsuits. (Both, courtesy of the Library of Congress.)

Eleventh Annual Bathing Girl Revue.
August 2, 3, 4, 5, 6, 1930.

Maurer, Copyright, 1930.

In June 1929, the Fourth International Pageant of Pulchritude included a popular contestant from Brazil. Olga Bergamini de Sa arrived in Galveston on June 6. The other participants met her at the station with local dignitaries. She was accompanied by her mother, who acted as her chaperone. Miss Brazil was a charming and exotic beauty joined by representatives of France, Spain, England, Romania, Luxembourg, Austria, Holland, and Germany. She was not the first-place winner, and her painful loss was well documented. Consequently, Brazil never sent another contestant to the competition. The 1929 winners were Irene Ahlberg of New York as Miss United States and Lisl Goldarbeiter of Austria as Miss Universe. (Courtesy of Library of Congress.)

Dorothy Goff is captured here with a beautiful smile and striking pose. She went on to win the title of Miss Universe 1930. (Courtesy of Galveston County Museum.)

The lineup of 1930 finalists is in front of an oversized image of the planet earth and surrounded by mysterious clouds to mimic the universe. Participants came from all over the world to compete. Winner Dorothy Goff is depicted in the center of the photograph. In 1931, the pageant ended with Ann Lee Patterson of Northern Kentucky winning Miss United States and Netta Duchateau of Belgium being crowned Miss Universe. (Courtesy of Library of Congress.)

Dallas bathing beauty Marylee McElvany Shanks poses on the West Beach dunes in 1958. As the years passed, Galveston continued as a popular place for early summer outings, vacations, and bathing beauty events. (Courtesy of Jami Durham, Private Collection.)

This lineup of 1963 summer bathing beauties shows the Burns family, all from the Houston area, enjoying a day on the beach. Swimsuits were still shapely and fit for all ages of women. Pictured from left to right are "Mama" Celesta, Fay, Doris, Dean, and Christine Burns. (Courtesy of Debbie Morris, Private Collection.)

In 2009, the Islander By Choice, LLC (IBC), reintroduced the bathing beauty revue. Known as the Galveston Island Beach Revue, the event is hosted on the beach near the Hotel Galvez and more recently by the San Luis. The competition held in May is lively and colorful. Contestants in the new revue wear costumes, either vintage or contemporary. Men and women are invited to participate. (Photograph by David Canright.)

The IBC Galveston Island Beach Revue winners in 2012 are, from left to right, (first place) Alana Anderson of San Antonio, Texas; (second place) Callie Mulkey of Rockwell, Texas; (third place) Erin Haynes of Memphis, Tennessee; (fourth place) Leslie Thompson of Carrolton, Texas; (fifth place) Dana Blue of Galveston Island; and (crowd favorite) Megan Carpenter of Galveston Island. (Courtesy of Islander By Choice, Candace Dobson.)

An aerial view of Sea Arama Marineworld in 1965 shows the circular Oceanarium, the centerpiece of the park, with the man-made ski lake to the north. When the park opened, admission was $2.25 for adults and $1.75 for students. (Courtesy of Tim Gould, Private Collection.)

OPPOSITE: The 1,000-seat Aquarena stadium was home to many of the park's performing marine mammals, including dolphins Alpha, Connie, Lucky, Hastings, and Haley, seen here performing in the 1980s. (Courtesy of Tim Gould, Private Collection.)

SIX

SEA ARAMA MARINEWORLD

Sea Arama Marineworld, one of the nation's first ocean-themed amusement parks, opened its doors in Galveston in 1965 and quickly became the top tourist attraction on the island. Situated on 40 acres located between Ninety-first and Ninety-fifth Streets and Stewart Road and Seawall Boulevard, the 25-acre theme park featured an Oceanarium; a 1,000-seat stadium for orca, dolphin, and sea lion shows; exotic birds, snake and reptile houses; and a man-made four-acre ski lake for water-skiing exhibitions. A spectacular magnet for tourists, Sea Arama drew visitors from a multistate region, increasing year-round tourism for Galveston Island.

Sea Arama was conceived by Jack Dismukes, Austin businessman and president of Galveston Marine Aquarium Incorporated. Dismukes chose Galveston for the park's site because of the abundance of natural sea life and salt water, its proximity to the greater Houston metropolitan area, and the cooperation of Galveston's citizens and city government, who helped to develop the project. With the opening of Sea Arama, the city of Galveston took yet another step toward becoming the leading playground and recreational area of the entire Southwest.

In consultation with Marineland in Florida, Austin architectural firm Winfred O. Gustafson designed the park. Construction of the modernistic structures was overseen by architectural engineer

Kenneth E. Zimmerman, known for his work on Houston's Warwick Hotel and the Astrodome.

The $2-million facility opened to the public on November 7, 1965. Crowds of more than 2,000 people forced Sea Arama to stage four trained porpoise shows—twice the scheduled number—because the 1,000-seat amphitheater could not fit all the visitors at the two scheduled performances. Visitors also viewed marine specimens native to the Texas coast and exotic varieties from tropical seas in a 170,000-gallon Oceanarium and in beautifully illuminated jewel aquarium tanks along its outer edge.

By 1980, more than 4,275,000 paid guests had experienced Sea Arama Marineworld with an average annual attendance of 305,000 paid visitors. That year, general manager Dale Ware oversaw minor renovations of the park and added a new dimension to the show package with the addition of "The Jungle Fantasy Wild Cat Show."

Galvestonians were proud of the fact that their park had the largest number of different shows of any sea-life park in the United States.

In 1984, Galveston Marine Aquarium Incorporated sold Sea Arama to two Galveston real estate brokers, who spent close to $2 million on park improvements. In August 1986, the brokers announced a 10-year plan for $100 million in park improvements, including construction of four hotels and a recreational complex. Their vision included the ability for Sea Arama guests to take a tram to Moody Park, located on Offatts Bayou, where they could board a paddle wheel boat that would take them to Galveston's historic downtown. Within three months of their announcement, foreclosure notice was filed against the brokers for default of payment on a promissory note held by Dismukes and the original owners. In a last-minute agreement to keep Sea Arama open, original owners Jack Dismukes and Henry Ramsey bought the park back.

By the late 1980s, Sea Arama's facilities were showing signs of deterioration and a decline in attendance was noted after the opening of Sea World in San Antonio in 1988. Faced with rising costs, lower attendance, and the need to invest in major park renovations, the decision was made to close the park. The last Sea Arama Marineworld show was held on January 14, 1990.

Sea Arama's marine life found homes in other facilities. For several years after the park closed, the main aquarium, saltwater mammal pools, and other facilities were leased to local research and public education institutions. In 2006, the ghost remnants of the once state-of-the-art structures were demolished, leaving nothing in their place but the fond memories of millions of visitors.

The photographs in this chapter are courtesy of Tim Gould and the *Remembering Sea Arama Marineworld* website www.seaarama.zoomshare.com.

One of the most popular attractions during the warmer months of the year was the water-skiing exhibitions. The majority of the performers were local high school and college students. (Courtesy of Tim Gould, Private Collection.)

Trace Terrific, one of the park's oldest and largest porpoises, leaps high in the air during the grand finale of the show. Popular with visitors, the porpoise show was presented five times a day during the busy summer months. (Courtesy of Tim Gould, Private Collection.)

One of the most popular attractions in the park was the dolphin feeding tank, which allowed visitors to purchase fish to feed the dolphins. (Courtesy of Tim Gould, Private Collection.)

Mamuk, a 2,300 pound, 13-foot orca, takes a fish from the hand of trainer Ken Beggs. At the time, Sea Arama was one of only four marine parks in the world to have a killer whale. Mamuk was purchased by Sea Arama in 1969. His presence required a new $66,000 holding pen, 13 feet deep and 50 feet long, containing 80,000 gallons of water. (Courtesy of Tim Gould, Private Collection.)

During the "Dive to the Deep" show in the 200,000 gallon Oceanarium, visitors watched through 32 viewing ports below the water's surface as divers hand-fed giant groupers, stingrays, exotic barracudas, sharks, and dolphins. The main tank of the Oceanarium was surrounded by jewel tanks along its outer edge, with each tank holding different marine species from around the world. (Courtesy of Tim Gould, Private Collection.)

In 1980, John Campolongo (seen here) joined the Sea Arama family with his "Jungle Fantasy Wild Cat Show." The show featured Bengal tigers, Siberian tigers, a spotted leopard, a black panther, and three African lions. (Courtesy of Tim Gould, Private Collection.)

Campolongo was famous for having presented big cat shows around the world. He is seen here performing in 1980 with two of his tigers. Note Campolongo's German Shepherd dog in the ring under the tiger on the left. (Courtesy of Tim Gould, Private Collection.)

During the winter, the ski area was used for the "Noah's Ark" show. Led by trainer Brandy Smith in the 1970s, roller-skating tropical birds and the famous cockatiel from the television show *Baretta* performed on a floating stage in front of the 1,500-seat stands. (Courtesy of Tim Gould, Private Collection.)

Hal Newsom worked with the park's reptiles. During the daily snake shows, Newsom worked with both rattlesnakes and cobras. The grand finale of the show was the "Kiss of Death," depicted here. Newsom went on to do guest appearances on numerous television shows and theme parks. (Courtesy of Tim Gould, Private Collection.)

Sea Arama audiences were enthralled with the park's 10 American alligators and one crocodile. One of the park's alligator wrestlers, Bobby Andresakis, is seen here wrestling the park's 13-foot alligator, believed to be the largest in captivity in Texas at that time. (Courtesy of Tim Gould, Private Collection.)

Jones the sea lion is seen giving his trainer a hug, c. 1970s. The sea lion show was choreographed to music and pleased audiences with every performance. (Courtesy of Tim Gould, Private Collection.)

Tim Gould joined the Sea Arama staff as a specialized animal trainer in 1987, working mainly with seals, sea lions, and the dolphins. He is seen here feeding sea lions Constance and Tuna in the late 1980s. (Courtesy of Tim Gould, Private Collection.)

After the park closed in 1990, Gould, seen here with Oliver the sea lion, stayed on as part of a skeleton crew to care for the animals and continued their daily training until they had been placed in other parks. Today, Gould administers the *Remembering Sea Arama* website, and in June 2012, he organized a successful reunion of Sea Arama employees at the Moody Gardens Aquarium Pyramid. (Courtesy of Tim Gould, Private Collection.)

The 1839 Samuel May and Sarah Williams House was threatened in the 1950s with neglect and possible demolition. The newly formed Galveston Historical Foundation (GHF) purchased the house and would later restore it and operate it as a museum. (Courtesy of Galveston Historical Foundation's Preservation Resource Center.)

OPPOSITE: GHF began the annual Historic Homes Tour in 1974 as a way to bring recognition to the island's historic properties. It eventually was extended to the first two weekends in May. (Photograph by David Canright; courtesy of Galveston Historical Foundation's Preservation Resource Center.)

SEVEN

HISTORIC GALVESTON DISCOVERED

By the second half of the 20th century, Galvestonians began to recognize the fecundity of heritage tourism. They understood that the exceptionally large number of historic, late-19th century buildings in significant concentrations were easily historic districts that could be used to promote tourism. These leaders looked to the old Southern cities of Charleston, Savannah, and New Orleans that had established historic districts and well-known museums and historical attractions. While a number of organizations and individuals saw the potential of heritage tourism about the same time, the Galveston Junior League, Galveston Historical Foundation (GHF), and Galveston County Cultural Arts Council initially led the community's efforts.

In 1954, Ann Brindley, Katharine Randall, and others formed the Galveston Historical Foundation as part of a statewide effort to set up nonprofits to support preservation programs. The initial organization focused on Galveston County, but it eventually settled its attention on the island. GHF's most notable new focus was to buy (as needed) and preserve historic buildings, something quite different at the time. Its major effort was to purchase the threatened 1839 Samuel May and Sarah Williams House, the home of one of Galveston's founders, and later to open the house as a museum.

The Galveston Historical Society existed at the same time and traced its beginnings to 1871. The society leadership and membership mirrored that of the foundation and thus the two merged in 1958. In the early 1960s, Galveston preservationists worked with state representative 'Maco Stewart to introduce legislation creating an "Old and Historic District" in the East End neighborhood much like Vieux Carre in New Orleans. It was introduced in the Texas Legislature but failed to pass.

GHF went on to aggressively document Galveston's historic buildings with John Garner of the National Park Service's Historic American Building Survey in 1966 and then, within a few years, with the field survey work of the Texas Historical Commission. During the 1960s, Howard Barnstone, a noted Houston modernist architect, wrote an acclaimed book *The Galveston That Was* using photographs taken by Henri Cartier-Bresson and Ezra Stoller. This publication created awareness and stimulated the historic preservation movement in Galveston. In 1969, the Junior League of Galveston County purchased the Trueheart Building at 212 Twenty-second Street and restored it. The earlier architectural surveys were later used to create historic districts, including the East End in 1971 and Strand Mechanic soon thereafter. GHF leadership was largely made up of residents associated with the medical school or who had a familial association with Galveston's historical development, in particular the Moody and Kempner families.

The Galveston County Cultural Arts Council hired Emily Whiteside in the early 1970s, and GHF hired its first executive director, Peter Brink, in 1973. The arts council in turn hired an important preservation consultant, Ellen Beasley, in 1973 who would document more historic properties and prepare a model report for the American bicentennial celebration. Under the banner of the American bicentennial to be celebrated in 1976, the arts council progressed in its vision to remake the island's arts using historic buildings and resources while GHF created several historic districts of national significance, a revolving fund to preserve buildings on the Strand, and continued restoration of Williams and Ashton Villa house museums. GHF also initiated two major community events: Dickens on the Strand and the annual Historic Homes Tour.

The organization expanded into preservation of maritime history in the late 1970s and purchased, then restored, the 1877 iron barque *Elissa*. Emily Whiteside, director of the arts council, led an ambitious effort to purchase and restore the Grand Opera House in the 1970s as well as rehabilitating a downtown building in the early 1970s as a loft. Her efforts resulted in making the 1894 Grand Opera House one of the city's most notable attractions.

These forward-thinking Galvestonians envisioned an island where history and architecture would contribute to the local economy as well as preserve properties, vessels, and sites for future generations. As the island moved into the 21st century, heritage tourism played a significant role in the local economy and complemented the beach, seawall, special events, and attractions already at work in Galveston.

The Williams House, later known as the Williams-Tucker House, proved a successful model of an American house museum during the 1970s and 1980s. By 2007, however, visitation dropped below 1,200 a year and GHF discontinued operating it as a full-time museum. (Courtesy of Galveston Historical Foundation's Preservation Resource Center.)

The 1892 Walter and Josephine Gresham house opened as a house museum in 1963 under the ownership of the Galveston Houston Archdiocese. Bishop Byrne lived in the house while in Galveston, but after his death, it was no longer needed by the diocese. Local preservationists worked with the diocese to open the house as a museum. (Photograph by David Canright; courtesy of Galveston Historical Foundation's Preservation Resource Center.)

Galveston Historical Foundation worked for several years for a means of saving Ashton Villa when the El Mina Shrine Temple put the building and grounds up for sale. GHF eventually worked with a federal government Urban Development Action Grant of the 1970s to have the city purchase the house as an economic development (heritage tourism) initiative. (Courtesy of Galveston Historical Foundation's Preservation Resource Center.)

This candid photograph captures three unlikely preservationists. From left to right are Houston architect and author of *The Galveston That Was* Howard Barnstone, internationally acclaimed architect Phillip Johnson, and GHF director Peter Brink. The decorative ironwork of Ashton Villa became the model that Johnson used in the Cresent Hotel in Dallas. (Courtesy of Galveston Historical Foundation's Preservation Resource Center.)

This 1979 photograph, taken inside Ashton Villa after being opened as a house museum, captures early preservationists, from left to right, Jean Mills, Peter Brink, Sally Wallace, Katharine Randall, Inez Lassell, Harry Levy Jr., and Judy Schiebel. (Courtesy of Galveston Historical Foundation's Preservation Resource Center.)

The Mary Moody Northen Endowment opened the Moody Mansion for tours in 1991. The house became the fourth house museum for Galveston and recognizes the history and contributions of the Moody family. (Courtesy of Galveston Historical Foundation's Preservation Resource Center.)

The 1838 Menard House is the island's oldest extant residence. The home of Michel Menard, a founder of Galveston, the property is today managed by GHF as a rental venue and educational complex recognizing the island's earliest history. It is opened on special occasions with lectures, tours, and event rentals. (Courtesy of Galveston Historical Foundation's Preservation Resource Center.)

Emily Whiteside, director of the Galveston County Cultural Arts Council, purchased this building at 217 Tremont Street to create the first downtown residential loft. Also in the photograph is O'Neil Ford, principal architect with Ford, Powell & Carson in San Antonio, who designed the loft conversion. (Courtesy of Galveston Historical Foundation's Preservation Resource Center.)

The arts council worked hard in the 1970s to bring attention to downtown and the Strand. This photograph shows Lennie Moscowitz, an artist, working in his loft studio under the observation of preservationist Dr. Burke Evans. (Courtesy Dr. Eric Avery, Private Collection.)

George and Cynthia Mitchell stand in front of the Leon & H. Blum Building that became the Tremont Hotel in 1985. The Mitchells provided much vision and support in their rehabilitation of historic buildings on the Strand and Mechanic Street. (Courtesy of Galveston Historical Foundation's Preservation Resource Center.)

George Mitchell's first preservation project was the purchase of the T.J. League Building at 2301 Strand from Galveston Historical Foundation. Boone Powell of Ford, Powell & Carson managed the rehabilitation into lofts, shops, and a restaurant. The building housed the Windletrap Restaurant, a popular establishment in the early revitalization of the Strand. (Courtesy of Galveston Historical Foundation's Preservation Resource Center.)

A candid photograph of Strandfest in 1977 caught the early rehabilitation project of Jack King. This became King's Confectionery, with ice cream and candies, and remains a popular attraction on the Strand. (Courtesy Adrienne and Michael Culpepper, Private Collection.)

In 2009, on the first anniversary of Hurricane Ike, Galveston Historical Foundation initiated a Revival Race, beginning and ending downtown. This photograph shows runners leaving the starting line at the Tremont Hotel. (Photograph by David Canright; courtesy of Galveston Historical Foundation's Preservation Resource Center.)

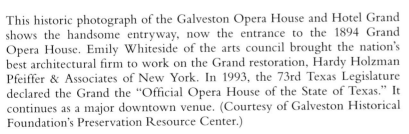

This historic photograph of the Galveston Opera House and Hotel Grand shows the handsome entryway, now the entrance to the 1894 Grand Opera House. Emily Whiteside of the arts council brought the nation's best architectural firm to work on the Grand restoration, Hardy Holzman Pfeiffer & Associates of New York. In 1993, the 73rd Texas Legislature declared the Grand the "Official Opera House of the State of Texas." It continues as a major downtown venue. (Courtesy of Galveston Historical Foundation's Preservation Resource Center.)

The Strand revitalization is transforming into a community gathering place, including the annual Lone Star Biker Rally. This 2012 photograph shows the bikers using all aspects of the Strand. (Photograph by David Canright; courtesy of Galveston Historical Foundation's Preservation Resource Center.)

Galveston Historical Foundation began the annual Dickens on the Strand holiday event in 1973. Evangeline Whorton, a longtime volunteer of GHF, conceived of this event to recognize the works of Charles Dickens and to bring attention to an extraordinary collection of historic buildings on the Strand. The event held the first weekend of December includes a descendant of Charles Dickens, parades, entertainers, food, and charming costumes, including those worn by a modern-day Queen Victoria. (Photograph by David Canright; courtesy of Galveston Historical Foundation's Preservation Resource Center.)

In 2009, Galveston Historical Foundation began a new event remembering the Battle of Galveston, which occurred on January 1, 1863. The battle was one of the few Civil War events to occur in Texas but was a decisive win by the Confederate army. (Photograph by David Canright; courtesy of Galveston Historical Foundation's Preservation Resource Center.)

In 1985, George Mitchell brought the historic Mardi Gras celebration back to Galveston. Parades, balls, and special events highlight the Mardi Gras season and bring thousands to the island. This photograph shows the Quaker City String Band Philadelphia Mummers, led by Bob Shannon, in the Knights of Momus parade. (Galveston Island Convention and Visitors Bureau.)

The harbor took a new look in the early 1990s with the development of Pier 21, completed by Cynthia and George Mitchell. Ford Powell & Carson of San Antonio transformed this working harbor into a complex of restaurants, hotel, the Pier 21 Theater showing the *Great Storm Experience*, and a small marina. (Galveston Island Convention and Visitors Bureau.)

Galveston Historical Foundation brought the historic 1877 iron barque *Elissa* to Galveston in 1979. This project, led by local preservationists, sought to develop an understanding of the maritime heritage and create a new attraction. This photograph shows *Elissa* arriving at Galveston with an anxious crowd on the dock. In 2005, the 79th Texas Legislature declared *Elissa* the "Official Tall Ship of Texas." (Courtesy of Galveston Historical Foundation's Preservation Resource Center.)

GHF made *Elissa* and the Texas Seaport Museum a major local tourist attraction by 1990. The 1877 iron barque is open for tours as is the museum. This interesting photograph shows a cruise ship passing *Elissa* in 2011. Several major cruise ship lines call Galveston home. (Courtesy Galveston Island Convention and Visitors Bureau.)

In 1997, the Offshore Energy Center created the Ocean Star exhibit near Pier 19 on the harbor front. The exhibit informs approximately 40,000 visitors a year from across the nation and around the world about oil and gas exploration in the Gulf of Mexico. (Courtesy of Offshore Energy Center.)

Galveston Historical Foundation acquired the *Seagull II* in 2004 as a way to expand educational programs of maritime resources in the bay. The *Seagull* leaves from Pier 22 and Texas Seaport Museum daily. (Courtesy of Galveston Historical Foundation's Preservation Resource Center.)

After the demolition of the quarantine station on Pelican Island in the 1960s, the city acquired the small area on the far eastern end of the island for Seawolf Park. The Galveston Park Board developed the site as a fishing pier as well as a visitors' center. In the 1990s, a nonprofit organization formed to bring the USS *Cavalla*, a World War II submarine, to Seawolf Park as a tourist attraction. (Galveston Island Convention and Visitors Bureau.)

In 2005, Galveston welcomed Schlitterbahn as a new attraction near Moody Gardens on the island's west end. This water attraction is one of the island's most important year-round venues, featuring both outdoor and indoor water attractions. (Galveston Island Convention and Visitors Bureau.)

Preservation leader Sally Wallace (right) and consultant Ellen Beasley (left) are pictured in the historic 1880 Garten Verein Dancing Pavilion. Wallace is credited with saving the Hendley Building, 2000–2016 Strand, in the 1960s. She and her business partner, Joel Donovan, opened Hendley Market soon after. (Courtesy of Galveston Historical Foundation's Preservation Resource Center.)

Initiated in the 1980s and completed in 1992–1993, the Moody Foundation developed a major island attraction on the west end near Eighty-first Street. The 142-acre theme park is the design work of Morris Architects. The tourist attraction includes an IMAX 3D theater, a rainforest, aquarium, the Colonel Paddlewheel Boat, a hotel, and a convention center surrounded by landscaped outdoor recreation areas. (Galveston Island Convention and Visitors Bureau.)

ABOUT THE GALVESTON HISTORICAL FOUNDATION

Incorporated in 1954, the Galveston Historical Foundation (GHF) is one the nation's largest local preservation organization. During the past 50 years, the foundation has expanded its mission to encompass community redevelopment, public education, historic preservation advocacy, maritime preservation, and stewardship of historic properties. Today, the Galveston Historical Foundation has more than 2,000 memberships representing individuals, families, and businesses across Texas, the United States, and abroad and exerts a profound impact on the culture and economy of Galveston.

The work of GHF has earned the foundation recognition by prominent state and national organizations. Among the recognized efforts are the redevelopment of the Strand, the rescue and restoration of the 1877 iron barque the *ELISSA*, the revitalization of historic residential neighborhoods and creation of historic districts, and the conception of signature events, including Dickens on The Strand and the Galveston Historic Homes Tour.

Galveston Historical Foundation serves as the steward and operator of many of Galveston's most significant historic properties: the 1838 Michel Menard House, 1839 Samuel May Williams House, 1859 Ashton Villa, 1859 St. Joseph Catholic Church, 1861 US Custom House, 1880 Garten Verein, 1887 Tall Ship *ELISSA*, 1892 Bishop's Palace, 1937 *Santa Maria* Shrimp Boat, and Rosewood Cemetery.

The Galveston Historical Foundation continues to be a driving force in the development and enrichment of the city of Galveston. The foundation is major voice of preservation advocacy both locally and throughout the state. The Galveston Historical Foundation's many departments, programs, events, and volunteers are all dedicated to its mission: preserving and revitalizing the architectural, cultural, and maritime heritage of Galveston Island for the education and enrichment of all.

DISCOVER THOUSANDS OF LOCAL HISTORY BOOKS FEATURING MILLIONS OF VINTAGE IMAGES

Arcadia Publishing, the leading local history publisher in the United States, is committed to making history accessible and meaningful through publishing books that celebrate and preserve the heritage of America's people and places.

Find more books like this at
www.arcadiapublishing.com

Search for your hometown history, your old stomping grounds, and even your favorite sports team.